**SCHOLASTIC**

# Teaching With Favorite
# ALPHABET Books

Kama Einhorn

NEW YORK • TORONTO • LONDON • AUCKLAND • SYDNEY
MEXICO CITY • NEW DELHI • HONG KONG • BUENOS AIRES

**Teaching** *Resources*

*for Satya*

Book cover from EATING THE ALPHABET: FRUITS AND VEGETABLES FROM A TO Z by Lois Ehlert. Copyright © 1989 by Lois Ehlert. Reprinted by permission of Houghton Mifflin Harcourt Publishing Company.

Book cover from INTO THE A, B, SEA by Deborah Lee Rose, illustrated by Steve Jenkins. Illustrations copyright © 2000 by Steve Jenkins. Reprinted by permission of Scholastic Inc.

Book cover from I SPY A TO Z: A BOOK OF PICTURE RIDDLES by Jean Marzollo, photographs by Walter Wick. Photo compilation copyright © 2007 by Walter Wick. Reprinted by permission of Scholastic Inc.

"Name Chant" adapted from *September Idea Book* by Karen Sevaly. Copyright © 2007 by Teacher's Friend, a Scholastic Company. Used by permission of the publisher.

"B Is for Bear Biscuits" activity adapted from *Teaching With Favorite Mem Fox Books* by Pamela Chanko. Copyright © 2005 by Pamela Chanko. Reprinted with permission of the publisher.

Cover design: Brian LaRossa
Interior design: Kathy Massaro
Interior illustrations: Maxie Chambliss, Anne Kennedy, Shelley Dieterichs, and James Graham Hale

Text copyright © 2011 by Kama Einhorn
Illustrations copyright © 2011 by Scholastic Inc.

ISBN: 978-0-545-23695-9

Published by Scholastic Inc.
All rights reserved.
Printed in the U.S.A.

1 2 3 4 5 6 7 8 9 10    40    17 16 15 14 13 12 11

# Contents

# About This Book

Alphabet books are a favorite, familiar genre for children and teachers. Though their topics and formats may vary, most alphabet books present each alphabet letter with corresponding words and images. Like many teachers, you may already have a section in your classroom library devoted to ABC books.

## Using Alphabet Books in Your Literacy Instruction:

* Builds letter recognition
* Enriches and expands vocabulary
* Teaches letter sequence
* Teaches and reinforces sound-symbol correspondence
* Helps develop phonemic awareness
* Is good for children who may be intimidated by dense text
* Lets children say, hear, and see the whole alphabet in a variety of contexts
* Is great for English language learners

The activities in this book are designed to help you get the most out of using alphabet books in your classroom. You'll find detailed discussion guides to use before, during, and after reading each book, plus cross-curricular activities to extend children's learning. Page 6 provides general activities to enhance your study of alphabet books. On the pages that follow, you'll find activities to use with all 12 featured alphabet books (which span a variety of formats and topics). Each book unit includes:

* **About the Book:** An introduction to the book includes a brief synopsis.

* **Concepts and Themes:** See at a glance the central themes and concepts presented in the book.

* **Before Reading:** Each lesson begins with suggestions for introducing the book that build children's interest in the topic, activate prior knowledge, and encourage the use of previewing and predicting skills.

* **During Reading:** This section suggests areas of focus for a read-aloud, such as noticing details in the pictures, examining text features, discussing unfamiliar words, making connections to the story, and predicting what happens next.

* **After Reading:** Here you'll find discussion tips for helping children retell the story, relate it to their own lives, and review vocabulary, as well as tips for sharing the book on repeated readings.

* **Spotlight On. . . :** This section offers mini-lessons and activities that focus on a specific letter of the alphabet. (On the Contents page, you'll find the alphabet letters targeted for different books.)

❄ **Extending Learning:** Use these activities to reinforce and expand learning and make connections to other areas of the curriculum. Activities focus on literacy-related skills including phonemic awareness, letter recognition, letter formation, letter sequence, vocabulary, and reading comprehension, as well as cross-curricular links to math, science, social studies, art, dramatic play, movement, cooking, and following directions.

❄ **Literature Links:** Here you'll find a list of other books and other resources that relate to the unit's theme.

❄ **Reproducible Activity Pages:** Included in most of the units are ready-to-use pages, such as templates, manipulatives, writing frames, word and picture cards, and more.

# Connections to the Language Arts Standards

The activities in this book are designed to support you in meeting the following PreK–1 standards as outlined by Mid-continent Research for Education and Learning (McREL), an organization that collects and synthesizes national and state curriculum standards—and proposes what teachers should provide for their students to become proficient in language arts, among other curriculum areas.

### Uses the general skills and strategies of the reading process

- Knows that print and written symbols convey meaning and represent spoken language
- Knows the proper way to handle books, that print is read from left to right, top to bottom, and that books are read front to back
- Understands that illustrations and pictures convey meaning
- Uses meaning clues to aid comprehension and make predictions about content
- Knows some letters of the alphabet, such as those in the student's own name and some familiar words in print, such as own first name
- Uses basic elements of phonetic analysis to decode unknown words
- Understands level-appropriate sight words and vocabulary

### Uses the general skills and strategies of the writing process

- Knows that writing, including pictures, letters, and words, communicates meaning and information
- Uses drawings to express thoughts, feelings, and ideas
- Uses emergent writing skills to write for a variety of purposes and to write in a variety of forms

- Uses writing and other methods to describe familiar persons, places, objects, or experiences
- Uses knowledge of letters to write or copy familiar words, such as own name
- Uses writing tools and materials

### Uses listening and speaking strategies for different purposes

- Uses new vocabulary to describe feelings, thoughts, experiences, and observations
- Tells stories based on personal experience or make-believe
- Asks and responds to questions
- Makes contributions in class and group discussions
- Follows rules of conversation and group discussion
- Creates, acts out, recites, and responds to familiar stories, songs, rhymes, and plays
- Gives and responds to simple oral directions
- Knows rhyming sounds and simple rhymes and that words are made up of sounds and syllables
- Listens to a variety of fiction, nonfiction, poetry, drama, rhymes, and songs

SOURCE: *Content knowledge: A compendium of standards and benchmarks for K–12 education* (4th ed.). Mid-continent Research for Education and Learning, 2004 (http://www.mcrel.org/standards–benchmarks).

# Exploring Alphabet Books and Letters: Activities for Anytime

In addition to the teaching activities for each featured title in this book, try any of the following ideas to enrich and expand letter learning.

## Letter Cards

It's convenient to have a full set of alphabet cards in your classroom. Many of the activities in this book call for them. Have one set of uppercase, one set of lowercase, and one set that depicts both. (If desired, enlarge and photocopy the reproducible letters on pages 8–12 onto colored paper. Then affix them to separate index cards using a glue stick. To pair upper- and lowercase letters, glue one of each to larger index cards.)

## Sing It

Most children learn letter names not by seeing the letters, but by singing the traditional alphabet song (to the tune of "Twinkle, Twinkle, Little Star"). Each time you share an alphabet book, you might begin and end the lesson by singing this classic song. If you have an alphabet frieze displayed in the classroom, invite one child to use a pointer to follow along.

## Word Wall

At the beginning of the school year, create a bulletin board (or area on the wall) with each letter of the alphabet displayed. As you share each alphabet book, use index cards to write the words you encounter that begin with that letter. Display the cards under the corresponding letter. Refer to the wall periodically to review letter sounds.

## ABC Corner

Set up an area in which children can explore letters in a variety of ways. Provide letters to trace, a whiteboard and dry-erase markers, letter stencils and stamps, magnetic letters, letter cards, alphabet puzzles, and art supplies.

## Look for the Letter

When teaching a particular letter, for example, uppercase $D$, write it on chart paper or the whiteboard using a red marker. Then, using a black marker, scatter letters around it ($D$'s as well as other letters). Challenge children to look at the target letter in red, then find and circle its matches among the black ones.

## ABC Games

**Tic-Tac-Letters:** Play tic-tac-toe using letters other than $X$ and $O$.

**Dot-to-Dot Letters:** Use a whiteboard or chart paper to create dot-to-dot letters for children to trace.

**Alphabet Concentration:** Have children try to find matching upper- and lowercase letters using the letter cards on pages 8–12.

## Name Chant

Children will love this interactive chant that connects letter learning with their own names. It also helps build listening skills.

If your name starts with **A** or **B**,
put your right hand on your knee.

If your name starts with **C** or **D**,
stomp your foot to the count of three.

If it starts with **E**, **F**, or **G**,
bend down, jump up, and shout, "It's me!"

If your name starts with **H** or **I**,
with both hands, reach for the sky.

If it starts with **J**, **K**, or **L**,
make the sound of a ringing bell.

If your name starts with **M** or **N**,
go "Cluck, cluck, cluck!" like a hen.

If it starts with **O**, **P**, or **Q**,
Point to your left foot and left shoe.

If your name starts with **R** or **S**,
let us know by saying, "yes!"

If your name starts with **T**, **U**, or **V**,
make the sound of a bumblebee.

If your name starts with **W**, **X**, **Y**, or **Z**
pretend you are now a cute monkey.

Now, together, let's play this game,
when I say, "Go!" call out your name!

## More Favorite Alphabet Books

In addition to the titles featured in this book, try any of these ABC books to enrich and extend letter learning.

* *Alligators All Around: An Alphabet* by Maurice Sendak (Harper, 1962)

* *Alphabet City* by Steven T. Johnson (Puffin, 1999)

* *The Alphabet Tree* by Leo Lionni (Pantheon, 1968)

* *David McPhail's Animals A to Z* by David McPhail (Scholastic, 1988)

* *Dr. Seuss's ABC* by Dr. Seuss (Random House, 1963)

* *Farm Alphabet Book* by Jane Miller (Scholastic, 1987)

* *From Albatross to Zoo: An Alphabet in Five Languages* by Patricia Borlenghi (Scholastic, 1992)

* *The Graphic Alphabet* by David Pelletier (Scholastic, 1996)

* *The Handmade Alphabet* by Laura Rankin (Dial, 1991)

* *The Icky Bug Alphabet Book* by Jerry Pallotta (Charlesbridge, 1987)

* *It Begins With an A* by Stephanie Calmenson (Hyperion, 1993)

* *Miss Spider's ABC* by David Kirk (Scholastic, 1998)

* *Superhero ABC* by Bob McLeod (HarperCollins, 2006)

* *The Z Was Zapped* by Chris Van Allsburg (Houghton Mifflin Books for Children, 1987)

A B C

D E F

G H I

J K L

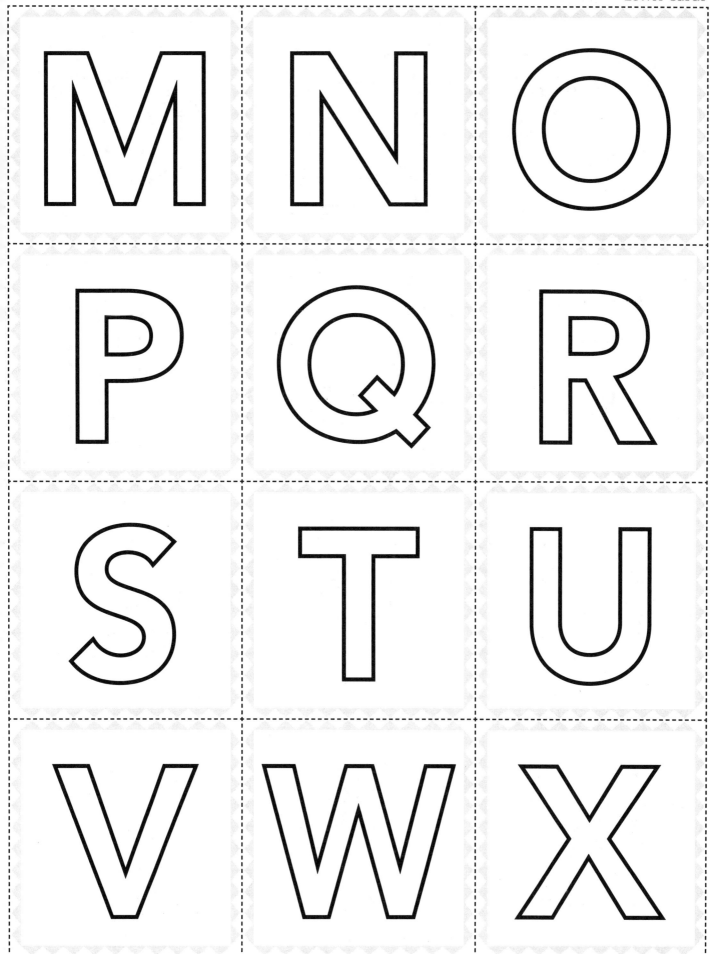

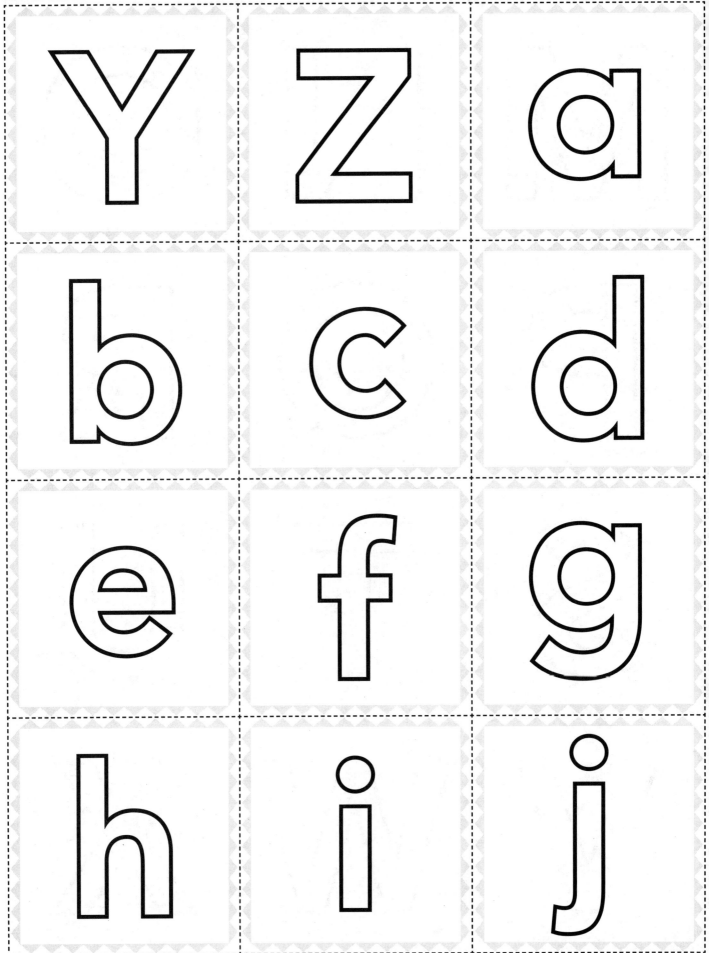

*Teaching With Favorite Alphabet Books* © 2011 by Kama Einhorn, Scholastic Teaching Resources

k l m

n o p

q r s

t

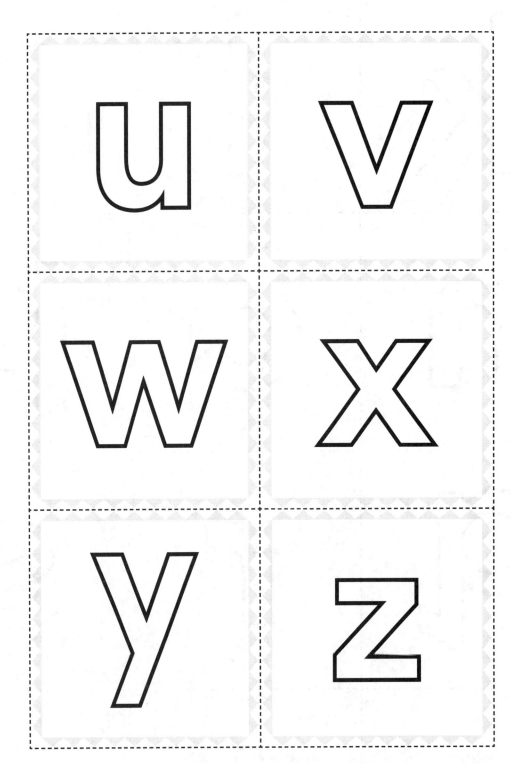

*Teaching With Favorite Alphabet Books* © 2011 by Kama Einhorn, Scholastic Teaching Resources

# Animalia

## By Graeme Base

(Harry N. Abrams, 1987)

It took Graeme Base more than three years to complete the illustrations for this visual treasure trove known for its intricate, meticulous details. Every page has a tongue twister, such as "Lazy lions lounging in the local library." Those lions look at books titled "Lassie Come Home" and "Let's Learn Latin" as a leprechaun, lizard, and lobster look on. You could share this book every week, all year long, and discover something new each time!

## Concepts and Themes

❉ Alliteration

❉ Fantasy & Imagination

❉ Noticing Details

❉ Diversity of Animal Life

❉ Uppercase and Lowercase Letters

## Before Reading

Begin by building children's interest in animals. Ask:

❉ What do you see on the cover of this book?

❉ Which animals can you identify on the cover?

❉ What do you think you might find on the pages of this book?

❉ What word do you see or hear in the title? (*animal*).
(Read the title aloud. Explain that "Animalia" means the entire animal kingdom—all animals.)

❉ Have you ever visited a zoo? What was the most interesting animal you saw there? What was it doing?

## During Reading

❉ Give children plenty of opportunities to get up close to each page. There are so many details packed into each piece of art, they are not likely to see them all upon the first reading! You might even focus on one page a day or week, allowing children to explore it in depth (or especially if you are focusing on a letter of the day or week).

❉ Ask children the main animal they see on each page. Then read aloud the alliterative sentence, emphasizing the beginning sound of the target word.

❉ Depending on children's age and level, they may only be able to grasp the main animal and one target word on the page. For instance, the *G* page shows "Great green gorillas growing grapes in a gorgeous glass greenhouse." If children can identify "green gorillas," that's fine. On later readings, you can explain what a *greenhouse* is, for instance.

❋ When necessary, discuss unfamiliar words children encounter in the text, such as *avoiding, basking,* and *crayfish.* There are some on each page, so use your own judgment about which words children need to know to understand the sentence. The illustration will usually aid comprehension, so you can point to various parts of the page as needed.

### After Reading

❋ Read the poem on the title page. The author invites the reader to find him in the book! It takes patience, but he's hiding on every page (in his red-and-yellow shirt). For instance, look at the middle of the *L* page, toward the bottom: he's on the cover of *Little Boy Lost.* (Turn the book upside down to see the boy right side up.) On the *E* page, we can only see his hand at the lower left of the page.

❋ Are there any animals that children are particularly interested in? Share books about that animal or look online for more information.

### Extending Learning

## Our Own Animalia (Phonemic Awareness, Letter Recognition, Art)

Each child can make his or her own page, focusing on an animal of his or her choice, to bind together into a class collaborative book.

1. Ask each child to choose an animal. It can be one from the book or any animal. Have children draw a picture of their animal.

2. Confer with each child and help her think of something her animal might be doing that begins with the same letter (for instance, a *dog dances* or a *rabbit runs*). Then help her think of other objects that begin with that letter to add to the picture (such as *donut, dot,* and *dish,* or *rose, rocket,* and something *round*).

A cute cat eats a cookie. — Jonah

3. Depending on grade level, write down the sentence as the child dictates it, or have her write it on her own. You can label the other items in the picture, too.

4. Gather all pages together into a class book and create a cover with the title, "Our Own Animalia." Share the book as a group, pointing out the different items that children have drawn on each page.

## Font Fun (Letter Recognition)

The pages in this book feature an eclectic variety of typefaces. Help children make sense of different versions of each letter and begin to notice environmental print in their everyday lives.

1. Page through the book, inviting children to examine the text. Some letters may be difficult to identify because they are so stylized.

2. Explain that the artist made all the letters look different to help tell the story. Look together at the *E* page. The word "enormous" is puffy and enormous! On the *G* page, the letters are carved into stone. On the *M* page, the letters are made to look like they have been created by a special computer. Explain that we see different typefaces (styles of letters) all around us every day.

3. Let children experiment with different typefaces on a computer. They can write their name and then try it in all different fonts and sizes, and print it out.

## Animalia Guessing Game

(Critical Thinking, Letter Recognition, Letter Sequence)

Build oral language skills with a "Twenty Questions"-style game.

1. Photocopy and enlarge page 17 and cut apart the cards. Gather children in a circle. Give one card to each child. (It's fine if your group has fewer than 25 children.) Tell children to not show anyone their card.

2. Choose one child to start. Invite children to ask that child questions to determine the animal on his card (his "secret animal identity"). For instance: "Do you have fur? What do you eat? Do you fly? Are you bigger than a person?"

3. When a child guesses the correct animal, the child whose "identity" was guessed puts his or her card face up in the center of the circle. Look at the card together and ask what letter the animal name starts with.

4. The child who guessed correctly goes next, with the group asking questions to determine that child's secret animal identity. Continue until the group has guessed everyone's animals. As you play, arrange the cards alphabetically in the center of the circle.

A is for *animal*, of course. How many animals can children find on the *A* page? (*armadillo, alligator, ape, ant,* and even an *alien!*) How many *A* foods? (*asparagus, apple, apricot,* plus an *artichoke* and an *avocado*). Write *Aa* on chart paper and make a list of all the words children find. Discuss the different sounds of *a* (long *a* as in *ape,* short *a* as in *alligator, r*-controlled *a* as in *artichoke*) and so on. To extend, write the words on separate index cards. Create a word wall with labels for the different sounds of *a.* Help children affix the word cards in the appropriate sections.

## Animalia Relay (Movement, Letter Recognition)

Invite children to act out the entire alphabet of animals!

1. Photocopy page 17 and cut apart the cards. Put all the cards in a box, bag, or basket.

2. Divide the group in half and mark a "Start" line on the floor with masking tape. Each team lines up behind the line. Place the basket between them.

3. Say "Go!" The first child on each team picks a card, reads the animal word, and moves the way that animal would move to the end of the room and back. Children can also use sounds to portray their animals.

4. When the child returns, the next player reaches into the box, bag, or basket for a new animal card. (Children can put their cards in a discard pile after their turn.) Continue until all the animal cards have been used.

## Animal Crackers

(Letter Recognition, Letter Formation, Letter Names, Phonemic Awareness)

Animal-shaped crackers are a great way to make letter-learning fun.

1. Bring in a box or bag of animal crackers. Ask children what they think will be inside. (Barnum's Animal Crackers™ typically feature: tiger, cougar, camel, rhinoceros, kangaroo, hippopotamus, bison, lion, hyena, zebra, elephant, sheep, bear, gorilla, monkey, polar bear, seal and giraffe, and koala; other brands will differ in variety).

2. Open the box and let a volunteer pick out a cracker and hold it up for all to see. Ask children to say its name and what letter it starts with. Write its name on chart paper, using a different color for the initial letter. Turn to that letter page in the book. Is that animal included on the page? Look closely on the page for other words beginning with that letter.

3. Then invite the volunteer to copy the initial letter next to the word. (The child can either trace a letter you have already written, or complete a dot-to-dot that you put on the chart paper.) Once the child finishes, he or she eats the cracker and another child has a turn.

4. Continue until each child has had a cracker. Since there will be more than one of each type animal in a box or bag, simply have children practice their letters near the words you have already written on the chart paper.

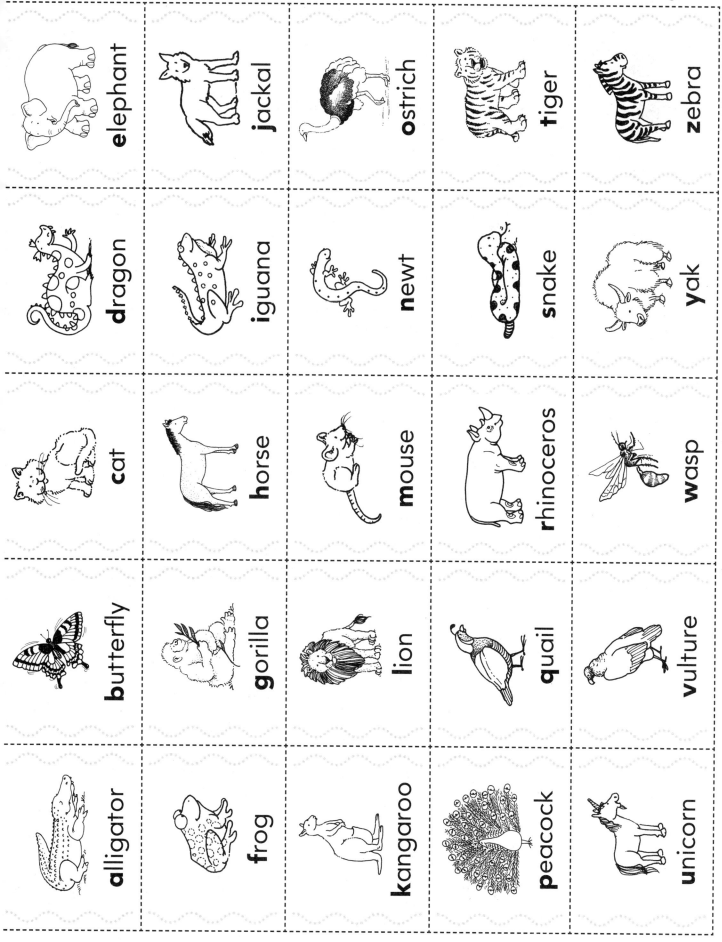

| | | | | |
|---|---|---|---|---|
| elephant | jackal | ostrich | tiger | zebra |
| dragon | iguana | newt | snake | yak |
| cat | horse | mouse | rhinoceros | wasp |
| butterfly | gorilla | lion | quail | vulture |
| alligator | frog | kangaroo | peacock | unicorn |

*Teaching With Favorite Alphabet Books* © 2011 by Kama Einhorn, Scholastic Teaching Resources

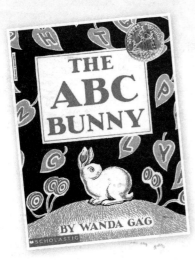

# The ABC Bunny

## By Wanda Gág

### (Putnam & Grosset Group, 1933)

## Concepts and Themes

⁕ Rhythm & Rhyme

⁕ Animals & Nature

⁕ Journeys

This classic Newbery Honor Book has delighted children since 1933. Whimsical, simple rhyming text bounces the reader through an alphabetical journey—then safely home again. Children naturally want to hop right along!

### Before Reading

Invite children to share any prior experiences they have had with bunnies. Ask:

⁕ Have you ever seen a bunny? Where? What did it look like? What color was it? What did its tail look like? Its ears?

⁕ What do rabbits and bunnies feel like?

⁕ What do rabbits and bunnies do all day?

⁕ What letter does the word *bunny* begin with? (Write an uppercase and lowercase *b* on the board or chart paper and have children air-trace the letters.)

Show children the cover of the book and read the title together. Ask:

⁕ What do you see on the cover?

⁕ What do you think this bunny will do in the pages of this book?

### During Reading

To aid in comprehension, point to the picture that corresponds with the text. For instance, on the *C* page, with *C is for crash*, point to the falling apple.

### After Reading

⁕ Invite children to retell the story by listing the different things the bunny saw on his journey. List children's responses on chart paper, highlighting the initial letter (for instance, *apple*, *frog*, *owl*).

- Play "Rabbit Rhymes." Have the group stand up as you read the book aloud again. As you read, draw out each line to help children anticipate the rhymes (there is at least one on each page). For instance, *M for Mealtime—munch, munch, munch. M-m-m! These greens are good for... lunch.* Tell children that every time they hear a rhyme, they should do the "bunny hop" (jump in place).

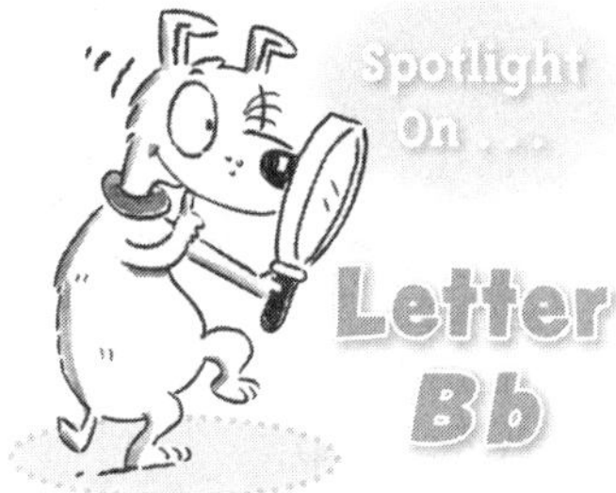


*B* is for *bunny*! Show children how to use their left hand to make a lowercase *b* by touching their index fingers and thumbs together to make a circle, and holding the rest of their fingers straight up, like the stem of the *b*. What happens if they do this with their right hands? (They'll form a *d*.)

Extending Learning

## The ABC Kids

(Letter Recognition, Letter Formation, Phonemic Awareness, Social Studies)

Your class can make a collaborative book—all about themselves and their own school day—using the same format as *The ABC Bunny.*

1. On the board or a piece of chart paper, write all 26 letters along the left side. Together, brainstorm words for each letter (words that describe what children do or experience all day long in school). For instance, *A is for adding, B is for books, C is for coloring.* Write a word next to each letter.
2. Assign each child one page to illustrate. (Depending on class size, some children may complete two pages, or two children can work together to complete one. One child can create a cover, as well.) Each page can include a simple sentence or two, such as "*B is for books.* We love to read." "*T is for Turtle,* who we feed every day." "*L is for Lunch.* We eat at 12:00." or "*P is for play.* We play hopscotch at recess." (Assist children in writing or have them dictate as you write, but encourage them to write the target letter themselves.)
3. Bind all of the pages together in ABC order to create a class alphabet book. Display it next to *The ABC Bunny* and read it together as a group.

## Rhyming Bunny-Rabbit Ears

(Phonemic Awareness, Vocabulary, Math, Science)

Children can play a matching game while building rhyming skills.

1. Photocopy page 21 and cut apart the ear patterns.
2. Ask children why they think rabbits' ears are long. Guide them to understand that rabbits can move their large ears around to hear better. See Lend An Ear, page 20, for an activity that lets children explore how rabbits hear.
3. Distribute one "ear" to each child. Check that each child can read the word on his or her ear. (You might say the word aloud as you hand it to each child.)

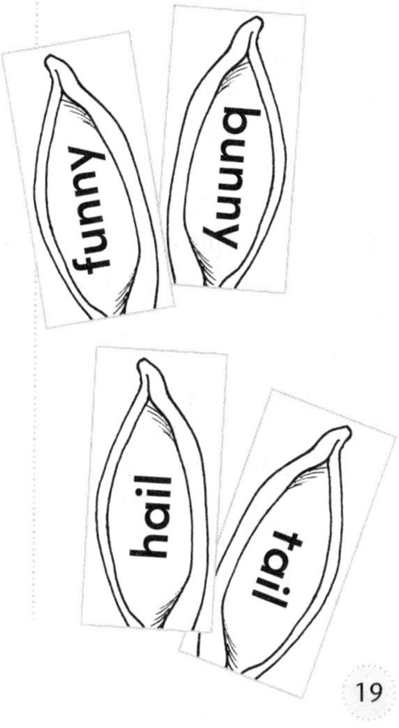

***Peter Rabbit's Hide and Seek ABC***
by Beatrix Potter
(Warne, 2004)

*A* is for apple, *B* is for butterfly, and *C* is for carrot (what else?). Here are Beatrix Potter's well-loved characters and classic illustrations in an interactive, guessing game format.

***The Runaway Bunny***
by Margaret Wise Brown, illustrated by Clement Hurd
(Harper, 1942)

First published in 1942 and never out of print, this classic tale of unconditional bunny love has soothed generations of readers with its reassuring words and sweet pictures.

***Wanda Ga'g, the Girl Who Loved to Draw***
by Deborah Kogan Ray
(Viking Juvenile, 2008)

A beautiful picture-book biography of this beloved author and illustrator, who began to draw as soon as she could hold a pencil. It begins with Ga'g's Minnesota childhood in a close-knit Bohemian immigrant community, where she supported her family with her artwork starting at the age of 15.

4. Tell children to find their match (the word that rhymes with theirs). Once they have, they stand together. When the whole group has finished, each pair should read their bunny-rabbit rhymes aloud to the group.

5. Count ears by 2's! How many ears altogether? How many "bunny-rabbits"?

## Lend An Ear (Science)

Children make rabbit "ears" to investigate how rabbits hear.

1. Show children a picture of a rabbit. Ask them to describe its ears. How are its ears different from theirs?

2. Give each child a large paper cup, cut in half. Have children hold the cup halves up to their ears. Invite them to whisper to each other, talk from various distances, and move the ears in different ways.

3. How do the cups change how they hear? *(Sounds seem louder.)* Ask children how they think this happens. *(The cups collect and direct sounds into the ears.)*

4. Discuss how big, movable ears help a rabbit keep safe from enemies. *(The long, cupped shape directs sounds into the rabbit's inner ears, helping it to hear better. A rabbit can also to point its ears in different directions to zero in on sounds from far away.)*

## Letter Leaves

(Letter Recognition, Letter Formation, Phonemic Awareness, Letter Sequence)

Build letter recognition upon repeated readings.

1. In advance, cut green paper into 26 squares (or leaf shapes) and use a red marker to write an uppercase letter on each.

2. Examine the cover of *The ABC Bunny* together. What do children see in the black sky around the bunny? (*Red letters on green leaves*).

3. Distribute one leaf to each child. (Say the letter names as you hand children their leaves.)

4. Read the book again. Emphasize the letter on each page and invite the child holding that letter to stand up as you read that page, showing his or her leaf to the group. You might also ask that child to repeat the line you just read. Continue until all children are standing.

5. When you are finished reading, challenge children to put their letters in an alphabetical row.

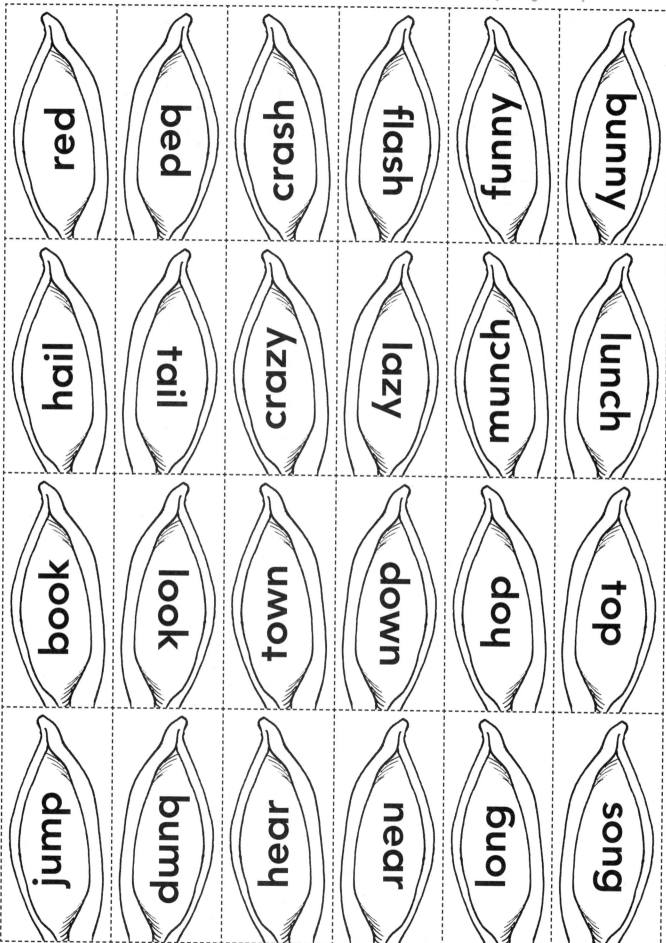

red   bed   crash   flash   funny   bunny

hail   tail   crazy   lazy   munch   lunch

book   look   town   down   hop   top

jump   bump   hear   near   long   song

# Ashanti to Zulu: African Traditions

### By Margaret Musgrove,
### Illustrated by Leo and Diane Dillon

### (Puffin, 1980)

## Concepts and Themes

- African Culture
- Cross-Cultural Awareness
- Uppercase Letters
- Proper Nouns

This Caldecott Medal-winning treasury of African traditions celebrates an enormous and varied continent. Each page focuses on a different African people's culture. For each people, luminous, detailed artwork depicts a man, woman, and child of the group, a typical shelter, an animal from the region, and an artifact and custom of the group.

### Before Reading

Begin by drawing on children's prior knowledge of Africa and sharing essential facts.

- Show children a globe. Point out where on the globe you are.

- Ask if anyone can locate Africa on the globe. Explain that Africa is a large continent made up of many different countries.

- Was anyone born in an African country? Has anyone ever visited Africa? Does anyone know someone who has? Give children the opportunity to share their experiences and what they know about Africa.

- Turn to the last page of the book and show children the map of Africa. The tribes that are included in the book are all listed on the map. Explain to children that they will be learning about each of these tribes—one for each letter of the alphabet.

### During Reading

- Read the paragraph on each page aloud, letting children examine the corresponding picture.

- Emphasize the beginning sound of the target word. Explain that the letter is shown in uppercase because the names of tribes are capitalized, just like the names of people, places like cities and towns, and names of schools.

- When necessary, pause to explain meanings of unfamiliar words that are key to understanding the text, such as *sacred, ancestors,* and *wiry.*

❋ Do children show a special interest in a particular culture or tribe? Research the tribe online or find other books for a more in-depth study.

❋ Point out the border on each page. It is a Kano knot, a design from North Niger in the 16th century.

**Extending Learning**

## Needs and Wants

(Social Studies, Letter Recognition, Phonemic Awareness)

The Lozi people travel by boat to higher ground every year when the Zambesi river floods, taking what they need. Help children think about this way of life and distinguish between needs and wants.

1. Write *Lozi* on the board or chart paper. Read the word aloud. Ask what letter and sound it starts with. Then read the *L* page again.

2. Tell children to imagine they are going on a boat, heading to an area far from home, and to think of all the things they will need to take with them to live outdoors. Children take turns naming one item they would take. Record their responses on chart paper or a whiteboard. (If possible, write or draw children's suggestions on cards or slips of paper.) Keep going until children have run out of suggestions.

3. Now explain that the boat has very little room! So you must choose six items from this list to take with you and leave the rest behind. Circle the items children choose; if using cards, sort them into "take" and "leave" piles.

4. As they decide which items to take and leave, help children think about the following: Are these things they will need in order to stay safe and healthy, or things they want but which are not necessary for their survival? Are there some other "needs" that they may have missed?

Spotlight On...

Letter
*C c*

Look at and reread the *C* page together. Explain that the letter *c* can sound different in different words, such as the hard sound in *cat, corn,* and *car* and the soft sound in *celery, city* and *celebrate*. When combined with *h,* the letter pair makes a whole different sound: *ch* as in *Chagga* and *children*. Make lists of words with hard *c*, soft *c*, and *ch*.

| | |
|---|---|
| (food) | stamps + envelopes |
| (blankets) | pencils |
| candy | paper |
| teddy bear | pots + pans |
| (water) | stove |
| (first aid kit) | video games |
| (flashlight) | TV |
| pillow | gum |
| books | computer |
| money | (tent) |

❄ The word foufou—meaning "pounding" because of the process in which it is made—comes from the Twi language, which is spoken in Ghana.

❄ Foufou is a staple in Western and Central Africa. Depending on the region, it can be made from yams, plantains, taro, cassava tubers or powder (and sometimes semolina, cornmeal, or rice).

❄ To make foufou, yams, plantains, or cassava are boiled, pounded until smooth, and then mixed quickly until the cooked vegetables become a thick, smooth paste. Traditionally, foufou is mixed with a long thin stick or a mortar and pestle.

❄ Africans have brought foufou all over the world. In North America, Africans might use potato flakes or Bisquick™ (see recipe at right).

❄ In the Caribbean Creole cuisine, foufou is made with plantains or cornmeal—and spelled foo-foo. And in Barbados, it has another name: coocoo.

## Foufou (Cooking, Phonemic Awareness)

The Ga people, living in the West African country of Ghana, make a food called *foufou* (or *fufu* or *foo-foo*) by pounding boiled white or yellow yams using long, thin sticks. The yams become smooth and pasty, and people roll it into balls, make an indentation in it, and dip it into stew or soup, using only their right hands. So foufou is both a food and a utensil!

1. Read the *G* page aloud again. What sound do children hear in *foufou*? (*f*)

2. Try the recipe for *foufou*, below, adapted for classroom use. While not authentic, it will give children an idea of what this popular Ga food is like.

3. When eating together, teach or reinforce concepts of right and left, challenging children to use only their right hands to eat.

### Foufou

This Foufou recipe, adapted for North American kitchens, makes six large foufou balls. They are easy to cut into quarters for a class-size treat. Enjoy with soup or stew, or eat plain.

#### Ingredients

- 6 cups water
- $2\frac{1}{2}$ cups instant baking mix (such as Bisquick™ or Jiffy Mix™)
- $2\frac{1}{2}$ cups instant mashed potato flakes

1. Boil the water in a large pot. Add the baking mix and potato flakes. Mix well with a strong wooden spoon.

2. Turn the heat down to medium and stir constantly for 1o to 15 minutes. (It's ideal if an adult holds the pot while children take turns stirring vigorously. Another adult should be on hand to supervise each child closely around the heat source.) The mixture will become very thick and difficult to stir, but keep going!

3. Fill a medium-sized soup or cereal bowl with warm water to wet its surface, then empty the water.

4. Spoon about one cup of the dough into the wet bowl. Shake the bowl quickly until the dough forms a smooth ball. Set your first foufou ball on a plate and repeat with the rest of the dough.

# We Are the Same, We Are Different

(Social Studies, Reading Comprehension)

The peoples depicted in the book are very different from one other and from people living in North America. But we are also the same in important ways. Help children develop their awareness of our common humanity.

1. Choose any one page to focus on. Closely examine the picture.

2. On chart paper, write three column headings. For instance, if you have chosen the *K* page, write *Kung People, Our Community,* and *Both.* Use a different color marker for each column.

3. Ask children what they see. What is happening in the picture? List their responses in the *Kung* column. Ask children what they notice about the Kung people that is different from them. List their responses in the *Kung* column and the *Our Community* columns as appropriate.

4. Then discuss similarities between the two groups and write those in the *Both* column.

| Kung People | Our Community | Both |
|---|---|---|
| Live in a place without much water | Live where water is easy to find | Take care of children |
| Hunt with bow and arrow | Buy food in supermarkets | Need water to drink |
| Store water in ostrich eggshells | Keep water in bottles or jugs | Carry bags on shoulders |
| People are short and wiry | People are all different sizes and shapes | |
| Use reeds to suck up water from ground | Use straws to drink | |

## Literature Links

**Africa Dream**
by Eloise Greenfield, illustrated by Carole Byard (HarperCollins, 1992)

In this lyrical tale accompanied by pencil drawings, an African-American child dreams of adventures all over long-ago Africa.

**A Is for Africa**
by Ifeoma Onyefulu (Puffin, 1997)

The author, who grew up in Nigeria and now lives in London, is a member of the Igbo tribe. She offers photographic images of traditional life and culture in her Nigerian homeland ("*K* is for Kola nuts offered to guests to show warmth and friendship"; "*S* is for Shaking hands").

**Jambo Means Hello: Swahili Alphabet Book**
by Muriel Feelings, illustrated by Tom Feelings (Puffin, 1992)

Another beautiful vision of African life, this time focused on East Africa.

**Why Mosquitoes Buzz in People's Ears: A West African Tale**
by Verna Aardema, illustrated by Leo and Diane Dillon (Puffin/Dial, 2004)

In this Caldecott Medal winner, Mosquito tells a story that causes a jungle disaster.

## Storytelling Traditions

The Ashanti people of Ghana in West Africa are known for their colorful folktales and mythology. Explore these tales and the rich oral tradition of these cultures with your class.

Explain that the role of storyteller in an African tribe is an important one. Folktales are stories that have been told over and over, from parents to children, to their children, to their children, and on and on, so the stories are very old.

## Storytelling Freeze (Social Studies)

We are all storytellers. Share the traditional Ashanti way of beginning and ending a storytelling session and have children tell their own stories.

1. Sit with children in a circle. Have children repeat after you, phrase by phrase, the traditional beginning to an Ashanti storytelling session: "We do not really mean that what we are about to say is true. A story, a story. Let it come, let it go."

2. Pick one child to begin telling a made-up story. After a few lines, say "freeze" and invite the next child to continue the story. Repeat all the way around the circle, with the last child telling the ending.

3. Then have children repeat the traditional ending to a session: "This is my story, which I have related. If it be sweet, or if it be not sweet, take some elsewhere, and let some come back to me."

## All About Anansi, the Spider

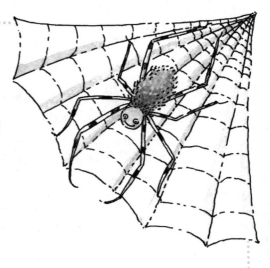

Anansi, the trickster, is one of the most important characters in West African folklore. In the Southern United States he has evolved into Aunt Nancy!

Anansi is a spider, but often acts and appears as a man. The character of Anansi is similar to the Coyote or Raven trickster found in many Native American cultures.

Stories of Anansi became such an important and well-known part of Ashanti oral culture that the word *Anansesem* ("spider tales") came to apply to all fables. Share some of the Ashanti people's Anansi stories:

* *Anansi and the Box of Stories: A West African Folktale* by Stephen Krensky, illustrated by Jeni Reeves (First Avenue Editions, 2008)

* *Anansi and the Lizard: A West African Tale* adapted by Pat Cummings (Henry Holt, 2002)

* *Anansi and the Moss Covered Rock* by Eric Kimmel, illustrated by Janet Stevens (Holiday House, 1990)

* *Ananse's Feast: An Ashanti Tale* by Tololwa Marti Mollel, illustrated by Andrew Glass (Sandpiper 2002)

* *Anansi Goes Fishing* by Eric Kimmel, illustrated by Janet Stevens (Live Oak, 1993)

* *Anansi the Spider: A Tale From the Ashanti* by Gerald McDermott (Henry Holt, 1987)

# Now I Eat My ABC's

## By Pam Abrams, photographs by Bruce Wolf

### (Scholastic, 2004)

Each letter in this book is a full-color photo made from real food, from the three crisp stalks of asparagus that form an uppercase *A* to the zig-zaggity zucchini sticks that make up *Z*. Whet children's appetite for letters by sharing these yummy pages and cooking up some literacy-building treats of your own.

## Concepts and Themes

- Uppercase Letter Forms
- Fruits & Vegetables
- Snacks

## Before Reading

Begin by looking at the cover of the book, building children's interest in these tasty letters and sharing fun facts. Ask:

- What do you see on the cover? What do you think you will find on the pages of this book?

- Who likes foods that...
     ...taste sweet, like cantaloupe or marshmallows?
     ...taste sour, like yogurt?
     ...taste bitter, like asparagus?
     ...taste salty, like French fries or pretzels?

## During Reading

- Let children examine the photo that represents each letter and say what it is made of. Read aloud, for instance, *A is for...* and let children complete the sentence with the word *asparagus*. Repeat the word, emphasizing its beginning sound.

- Have children use their index fingers to air-trace the letter in front of them as you examine each page.

## After Reading

- Page through the book again, asking children to think of other foods that begin with each letter.

- Together, examine the last page of the book on which the whole alphabet is presented. Ask children which letter they would most like to eat. Take an informal poll: Which letter looks the yummiest?

- Discuss any foods that children may not have seen before, such as *udon noodles* (a thick wheat-flour noodle popular in Japanese cuisine, usually served in hot broth) and *vanilla beans* (vanilla flavoring comes from these large pods).

## Spotlight On . . . Letter Ff

F is for *food*. . . and *fork*! Add plastic forks to the sand table and demonstrate how children can practice "writing" *F* and *f* in the sand using either end of the fork as a writing instrument. Add some to the art center, too, for children to use as painting or sculpting tools, or add plastic forks to the water table and discuss how they float.

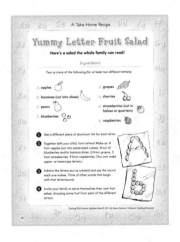

## Yummy ABC Song (Letter Names, Letter Recognition, Music)

Children can sing the traditional alphabet song, this time with a different ending!

1. Sing the traditional alphabet song with children, ending with the usual "now I know my ABC's, next time won't you sing with me?" Tell children they are going to learn another ending.

2. Look at the cover of the book. Can children read or remember the title, *Now I Eat My ABC's*? Have children sing these words after you: "Now I eat my ABC's, next time won't you eat with me?" Pantomime eating as you sing and invite children to do the same.

3. Page through the book together, inviting children to sing the alphabet song along slowly as they see each letter. Finish the song with the new ending!

## Now We Eat Our ABC's

(Letter Recognition, Letter Formation, Letter Names, Science)

Make some of these no-cook letters at snack time.

1. Tell children you are going to make letters just like in the book. The easiest, healthiest, and most classroom-friendly are: *A* (asparagus), *B* (blueberry), *C* (cantaloupe), *E* (eggs, using pre-cooked hard boiled eggs), *G* (grapes), *O* (orange), *P* (peas), *S* (strawberries), and *Z* (zucchini).

2. Spread large sheets of aluminum foil as your "canvas."

3. Look at the food you have gathered. Explain that fruits and vegetables are healthy snack choices. Point to each food. Which are fruits? Which are vegetables? Which are neither? (*egg*). See page 49 for an explanation of the difference between fruits and vegetables.

4. Form letters and display them at snack time so children can help themselves to a tasty treat.

5. Send home a copy of the recipe on page 30 for children to make with their families at home.

## Letter Pretzels (Letter Formation, Letter Recognition, Math, Cooking)

This easy recipe allows each child in your class to make and eat a different letter of the alphabet!

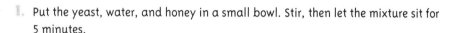

### Ingredients

- 2 tablespoons yeast
- 1 cup warm water
- 2 teaspoons honey
- 2 $\frac{2}{3}$ cups flour
- 2 teaspoons salt

Optional:
- coarse salt
- 1 egg, beaten with 1 tablespoon of water

1. Put the yeast, water, and honey in a small bowl. Stir, then let the mixture sit for 5 minutes.

2. Mix the flour and salt together in a medium bowl.

3. When the yeast mixture has expanded and is a little bubbly, add it to the flour and salt mixture. Stir the mixture, then finish combining with your hands until the dough is crumbly and flaky.

4. Put the dough on a cutting board and have children take turns kneading it into a ball.

5. Assign each child a letter. (Make sure all 26 letters of the alphabet have been assigned.) Then have each child break off a walnut-size piece of dough and roll it into a skinny snake. Children then twist the snake, or break it into pieces, to form their letter.

6. Place the 26 letters on a greased cookie sheet. Brush with egg and sprinkle with coarse salt, if desired. Bake at 325° for 10 minutes.

## Letter "Cookies" (Letter Formation, Letter Recognition, Letter Names)

Make these letter "cookies" to help children practice fine motor skills.

1. Give each child a rice cake and help him or her spread one tablespoon of cream cheese on it.

2. Let children choose the letter they want to form and a topping to "write" it (for example, blueberries, cereal, raisins, dried cranberries, thin pretzel sticks). Tell children to press the pieces of food into the cream cheese.

3. Have children sit in a circle and take turns showing the group the letter they made and saying its name and sound, before eating it.

### Alphabet Soup
By Scott Gustafson
(The Greenwich Workshop Press, 1994)

A host of animals attend Otter's housewarming party, bringing a wide variety of foods for his alphabetical soup. From Armadillo with his asparagus, to Zebra with his zucchini, they all contribute to a hearty meal and a lively alphabet book.

### Food for Thought
By Joost Elffers and Saxton Freymann
(Scholastic, 2005)

Ingenious food sculptures introduce shapes, numbers, colors, letters, and opposites in ridiculously clever and delicious ways.

### Up, Down and Around
By Katherine Ayres, illustrated by Nadine Bernard Wescott
(Candlewick, 2008)

How do vegetables grow? Every which way! This cheerful story is a colorful introduction to planting—and prepositions. Simple, quick-paced rhyming text follows vegetables from seed to table.

# Yummy Letter Fruit Salad

## Here's a salad the whole family can read!

### Ingredients

Two or more of the following (for at least two different letters):

- apples

- bananas (cut into slices)

- pears

- blueberries

- grapes

- cherries

- strawberries (cut in halves or quarters)

- raspberries

1. Use a different piece of aluminum foil for each letter.

2. Together with your child, form letters! Make an *A* from apples (cut into salad-sized cubes), *B* out of blueberries and/or banana slices, *G* from grapes, *S* from strawberries, *R* from raspberries. (You can make upper- or lowercase letters.)

3. Admire the letters you've created and say the sound each one makes. Think of other words that begin with that letter/sound.

4. Invite your family to serve themselves their own fruit salad, choosing some fruit from each of the different letters.

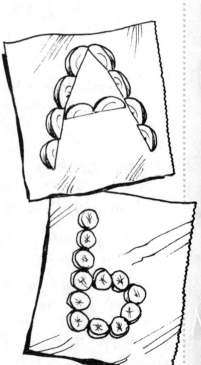

*Teaching With Favorite Alphabet Books* © 2011 by Kama Einhorn, Scholastic Teaching Resources

# I Spy A to Z:
# A Book of Picture Riddles

BY JEAN MARZOLLO, PHOTOGRAPHS BY WALTER WICK

(SCHOLASTIC, 2007)

The *I Spy* series builds on the traditional game, adding in whimsical rhymes and cleverly detailed photographs to create one great teaching tool. This book consists of favorite photographs taken from the entire award-winning series, with brand-new riddles to teach each letter of the alphabet.

## Before Reading

Show children the cover of the book. Ask:

* Who has played the game "I Spy"? How is it played? (Demonstrate: "I spy with my little eye…something green.")

* Who has played "Hide and Seek"? How is it played? (Explain that this book is a little bit like "Hide and Seek" because children will be looking for hidden things.)

* What does it mean to "spy"? (In this context, it is another word for "see.")

* What part of your face do you use to spy? (Have children blink their eyes a few times to "warm up" to the task. Say, "Get your eyes ready to spy!")

* What do you spy on the cover of this book? (Tell children to look closely and take their time. If children do not point out the letters themselves— the *G* covered in glitter, the *J* encrusted with jewels—point them out. Explain that they will find each letter of the alphabet inside.)

Look at the first spread in the book together (focusing on the letter *Aa*). Ask:

* Why are some of the letters printed in red? (Explain that each page, or spread, focuses on a different letter of the alphabet. Sometimes the letters are at the beginning of the word, as in most alphabet books, but in this book you can find them in the middle or even the ends of words, too.)

## During Reading

* Read the rhyme on each page aloud, emphasizing the sound of the target letter at the beginning, middle, or ending of words.

* Challenge children to find one thing listed in each rhyme. (Explain that they will revisit each picture upon later readings.)

### Concepts and Themes

* Beginning, Middle, and Ending Sounds (Phonemic Awareness)
* Lowercase Letters
* Visual Discrimination
* Noticing Details

❋ With each repeated reading, focus on a different letter/page. If you do letter of the day or week, this book is a great place to focus the learning.

❋ Write the target letter on chart paper for reference, reviewing the letter name and sound. You can easily get lost in the details of the photographs and spend a whole session on each page.

❋ Let children use plastic magnifying glasses to get closer looks at each page.

❋ Discuss unfamiliar words children encounter in the text, such as *antler*, *wick*, *spool*, and *evergreen*.

**Extending Learning**

## I Spy, You Spy

(Art, Letter Recognition, Letter Names, Phonemic Awareness)

Now is the time . . . to create your own rhyme! Children can create their very own "I Spy" pages.

1. Set out letter stamps, construction paper, glue, markers, crayons, and collage materials (toothpicks, paints, newspaper, magazine, or catalog cutouts, scraps of material cut into shapes, pipe cleaners, leaves, sticks, cotton balls or swabs, yarn, string or thread, paper plates, beads, buttons, sequins, glitter, tinfoil, photographs, paper clips, rubber bands, craft sticks, and so on).

2. Tell children to choose one letter to stamp on their collage, add items that begin with or contain that letter, then add other items as well.

3. When the collages have dried, help children complete the sentences below. Ask each child, "What do you spy?" Children can describe their creations to you as you write their words down as a dictation. If possible, help them use rhyming words at the end of each line. If their words happen to use the letter that they have stamped, point that out (you can use a different color, as in the book).

   I spy a _____, a _____, a _____,
   a _____, and the letter _____.

4. Have children share their collages with the group, challenging one another to find each other's hidden things and letters.

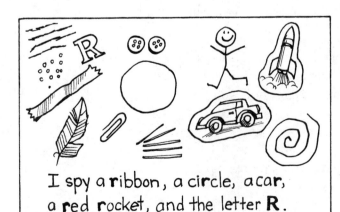

I spy a **r**ibbon, a ci**r**cle, a ca**r**, a **r**ed **r**ocket, and the letter **R**.

## Block Display (Vocabulary, Art, Phonemic Awareness)

You can get lost in this book's block structures! Using them as inspiration, children can create their own.

1. Examine the *B*, *F*, *G*, and *N* pages, plus the first *P* page, reading the rhymes aloud and finding the objects in each picture.

2. Ask, "What is the same about all of these pages?" (*They all show fanciful block scenes.*)

3. As a group, create a display in the block center with all different shapes, sizes, and colors of blocks (use letter blocks, too) and add any items you like—plastic figurines, and other small items—as in the book. You might ask children to take turns adding one block or item at a time until everyone has added to the structure.

4. Use a sheet of chart paper to write a class rhyme using words for items found in the display. Hang it near your creation. Use the same sentence frame as in the previous activity.

## Treasure Hunt

(Following Directions, Letter Recognition, Phonemic Awareness)

Use this activity with any page in the book to build spatial awareness and direction-following skills.

1. Select one child to be the "spy." That child stands close to the page with a pointer (you can use the eraser end of a pencil) on the very center of the picture.

2. Read the rhyme out loud. Select a target object from the picture for children to find and write the word for it on chart paper, highlighting the target letter. Read the word together.

3. The spy takes spoken directions from the group to find the object, using the pointer as he goes. Directions should use words and phrases such as *Start at the* [    ], *go right, go left, move up, move down, move over, closer to* [    ], *farther from* [    ], *it's near the* [    ], *it's behind the* [    ], and so on.

4. Let children take turns being the spy.

Spotlight On . . .
**Letter Ii**

*I* is for *I Spy*! Point out the letter *I* on the cover of the book. Demonstrate uppercase and lowercase *Ii* on chart paper and have children air-trace each. Tell children that when we write about ourselves, we always use uppercase *I*. Then examine the *I* page in the book together. Explain that the letter has two sounds, long *i*, which sounds like its name, as in "I spy a *die*," and short *i* as in *pig*, *wick*, *chick*, *gift*, and (*bowling*) *pin*. (Challenge children to find the picture of these items in the large photo on the page.)

# Number Boxes (Math, Phonemic Awareness)

Build numeral recognition and number sense at the same time.

1. Examine the *V* page and the *X* page, reading the rhymes aloud and finding the objects in each picture.

2. Ask, "What is the same about these two pages?" (*They both show boxes filled with numbers and items corresponding to each number.*)

3. Gather ten shoe box tops (or clean pizza box bottoms). You might have children paint them (each a different solid color). Arrange them on a table or in the center of the circle for all to see. Paint a large numeral on each (1 through 10).

4. Gather a variety of small objects around the classroom to sort into the boxes. Use the *V* and *X* pages in the book for reference. Here are some items you might use:

- a deck of playing cards
- dominoes
- magnetic numbers
- objects with a specific number of dots, stripes, or shapes on them
- blocks with a specific number of sides
- number cubes or dice
- beaded bracelets with a specific number of beads
- watercolor paint sets with a specific number of paint pots

5. Together, look at each item and decide which box it belongs in. You can add to this display all year long.

# I Spy Venn Diagrams (Phonemic Awareness, Critical Thinking, Math)

Venn diagrams can be a great way to help children sort, compare and contrast, and organize information. Even in the early years of school, Venn diagrams can be user-friendly, hands-on, and developmentally appropriate.

1. Examine the right hand *P* page and the *Y* page, reading the rhymes aloud and finding the objects in each picture.

2. Look at the *P* page. Ask, "What big shapes do you see in this picture?" (*Guide children to notice the overlapping circles.*) Trace the circles with your finger. Then turn to the *Y* page and ask, "How is this page similar to the page we just looked at?" Point out that they both show objects inside overlapping circles.

See page 47 for another Venn diagram activity.

3. Closely examine the *P* page together. Point to different items in each circle and ask children to describe what they see. Guide them to understand that the parts of each separate circle (the parts that do not overlap with other circles) contain objects that are similar in some way. Ask, "How are the items in each circle similar?" (*For example, the biggest section of the largest circle contains figures of people; the section of the circle on the lower left contains different kinds of sports equipment.*)

4. Now examine the overlapping parts of these two circles. Explain that this section shows what the objects in the two circles have in common—how they are the same. (*The overlapping section contains figures of people doing sports.*)

5. Repeat steps 3 and 4 for the *Y* page.

6. Lay out two circles made from yarn or string. Start by creating simple Venn diagrams using math manipulatives or any small figurines, toy cars, pattern blocks, plastic food, and so on. Here are two simple scenarios:

   • Group objects by color. In one circle, place three red objects and in the other, three yellow objects. Ask children to identify the sorting rule you used. To extend, overlap the circles and add one object that is both red and yellow. (Use whatever colors you have available.) Ask children to explain what the overlapping section represents (*objects that are both red and yellow*).

   • Use animal figurines to show animals that live on land and animals that live in water. Once children have had experience identifying the groupings in each circle, overlap them to create an area for animals that can live in both habitats. Invite children to help you place appropriate animals in the overlapping section.

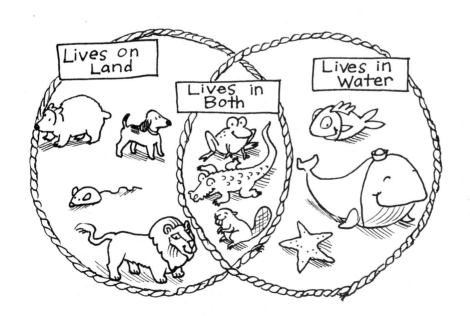

For multimedia *I Spy* fun and additional teaching resources, visit: scholastic.com/ispy

**Can You See What I See? Cool Collections**
By Walter Wick
(Scholastic, 2004)

Another mesmerizing photographic adventure from the co-creator of the *I Spy* series. Twelve picture puzzles feature intriguing assortments of just about everything. Great for teaching sorting and classifying.

**A Drop of Water**
By Walter Wick
(Scholastic, 1997)

Wick's striking color photographs of water in various states and stages of movement capture water drops, soap bubbles, water condensing and evaporating, snowflakes at 60 times actual size, frost, dew on a spiderweb, water as a prism, and more. Kid-friendly text accompanies each wondrous image.

**Where's Waldo?**
By Martin Handford
(Candlewick, 2007)

Continue to build visual discrimination skills and patience! Amidst the crowds of people on each bogglingly detailed page, readers must focus to spot Waldo.

# The Letters Are Lost

## By Lisa Campbell Ernst

(Penguin, 1996)

Follow a group of colorful alphabet blocks on an alliterative adventure that begins "Long ago the letters were all together, neat and tidy." Naturally, they all get lost! *B* fell into the bath, *H* was found under a hat, and *P* in a bowl of popcorn. Where are the rest? Children will delight in finding out on each page.

## Concepts and Themes

* Lost & Found
* Adventures
* Letter Sequence
* Uppercase Letters

Spotlight On **Letter Ll**

L is for *Letters* and *Lost*! Examine the *L* page together ("*L landed in a pile of Leaves.*") Can children find the ladybug on the page? Explain that some people think ladybugs are a sign of luck. Make a list on chart paper of more words beginning with *Ll*: *love, like, lollipop, lemon, lion, leopard, lump, lamp, left,* and so on. Children can "write" uppercase and lowercase *Ll* in the air with their fingers while saying the /l/ sound.

### Before Reading

Begin by activating children's background knowledge of the topic. Ask:

* Have you ever lost something? What was it?
* How did you know where to look for what you lost? Did you find it?
* Have you ever gotten lost yourself? Where did it happen? How did you feel?

Hold up a letter block. Ask:

* Has anyone played with letter blocks before? What can you do with letter blocks?
* How many sides on this block?

Show children the cover of the book and read the title aloud. Ask:

* What do you see on the cover?
* What do you think will happen in the pages of this book?

### During Reading

* Read the sentence on each page aloud, emphasizing the letter name and its beginning sound. ("*A flew high in an Airplane*").
* Challenge children to notice and name the other items on each page that begin with the target letter (for example, on the *A* page, they'll find an alligator).
* Have children air-trace each letter as you look at its page.

### After Reading

* Show children a set of letter blocks in order (as in the beginning of the story). Read the book again, picking up each letter block as you read about it. Put it behind you once it is "lost." Or, give each child a different block and invite him to hold it up as it is encountered in the text.

- Since only uppercase letters are shown, use chart paper to demonstrate the lowercase version of each letter.

- As you go, discuss unfamiliar words children encounter in the text, such as *tumbled, longed, admired, oval,* and *jig.*

- Examine the last spread, in which all the letters are assembled around the edge of the pages. Each letter has a clue telling where it has been (the *B* is wet from the bath, the *I* has ice cream smudges). Challenge children to remember what happened to each letter using these small visual clues.

### Extending Learning

## Letter Hunt
(Letter Recognition, Phonemic Awareness, Letter Names, Vocabulary)

The letters are lost, and it's up to children to find them—all over the classroom!

1. Ahead of time, assemble a full set of 26 letter blocks (or letter cards or magnetic letters). Before children enter the room, hide them around your space. Hide them in (or near, under, or behind) places that begin with the letter. See suggestions at right.

2. Challenge children to find all of the letters, bring them back to the circle, show their blocks, and say where they found them.

3. As the class looks at each letter block, emphasize the letter on the block, the sound it makes, and the location in which it was found.

## The Letters Are Lost: The Sequel
(Letter Formation, Letter Names, Phonemic Awareness, Vocabulary)

At the end of the book, the blocks are back together, but "not for long. Soon they will disappear again. Can you guess where they might go?" Here's an open invitation to have children make up their own scenarios!

1. Photocopy page 39 for each child and assign each child a letter. Help children brainstorm where their letters may be hidden. (*G* might be hidden behind a gorilla, *H,* under a hippo or in someone's hair.)

2. Have children illustrate their pages and help them write their letters in the "block." Then assist them in filling in and writing descriptions of where the letters were found. (For instance, *The letter A was found eating apple pie*; *The letter B was found playing with balls and bats*.) Bind the pages together, add a cover with the title, "The Letters Are Lost: Part 2," and read it together.

## Letter Hunt

- **A:** art center
- **B:** box, books, bowl
- **C:** cubby, carpet, cooking supplies, computer
- **D:** desk, door
- **E:** easel
- **F:** floor
- **G:** games
- **H:** hat (in dramatic play center)
- **I:** ice cube tray
- **J:** jar
- **K:** kitchen, pictures of kids
- **L:** library corner
- **M:** mat, math center
- **N:** number games (in math center)
- **O:** something orange
- **P:** painting supplies
- **Q:** quiet area
- **R:** refrigerator, rack, rug
- **S:** sink, shelf, science center
- **T:** table, tablecloth, toys
- **U:** utensils, umbrella, something upside-down
- **V:** plastic vegetables (in dramatic play/store area)
- **W:** water table, window, wall, writing center
- **X:** xylophone
- **Y:** something yellow
- **Z:** zipper (on clothing in dramatic play area)

**Literature Links**

### The Lost and Found
By Mark Teague
(Scholastic, 2001)

Two friends show Mona, the new girl in school, the "Lost and Found," hoping to help her find her lucky hat. When she disappears into the large box, the friends follow her—and explore an underground world filled with misplaced objects ranging from baby dolls to pirate treasures.

### The Turn-Around, Upside-Down Alphabet Book
By Lisa Campbell Ernst
(Simon and Schuster, 2004)

Bold graphics combine with an ingenious optical game. Each bright block letter appears within a box of color. Lines of text border each page, making the reader turn the book in a counter-clockwise circle to follow the words.

### Zinnia and Dot
By Lisa Campbell Ernst
(Viking, 1992)

Inside a chicken coop, squabbling hens get their feathers up over who is prettier and who has the best nest! But when confronted by a mischievous weasel, they put their cackling aside and problem-solve to decide what's best for their chicks.

# Block Center Letter Learning

(Letter Formation, Letter Recognition, Dramatic Play)

Add letter blocks to enrich the block center with literacy. Try some of these ideas:

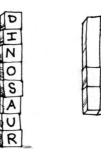

* Challenge children to spell certain words from the book by using letter blocks to build tall towers. Can they make the word before it topples?

* Children can also use regular wood blocks to create letter shapes. Challenge them to build letters very big. Which letters can stand up? Which lie flat?

* Challenge children to arrange all 26 letter blocks in alphabetical order in a big row on the floor.

* Have children build "stores" and "restaurants" from blocks and name them, making a sign from letter blocks.

* Add paper, crayons and markers, and tape for children to make signs for their buildings.

# Who's Got the Letter? (Reading Comprehension, Letter Recognition, Phonemic Awareness, Letter Sequence)

Build story recall and letter recognition skills with this activity.

1. Sit with children in a circle and give each child a letter block (or blocks) to hold. Without showing them the pages of the book, describe what happened on a random page without using the letter name but emphasizing its sound. ("Who has the letter that found a tower of *nnnnnnnumbers*?") Then the child with the *N* block puts it in the center of the circle, saying the letter name, *N*.

2. Continue until all the blocks are in the center of the circle. If children need help, write the letter on chart paper or show the page in the book, so children can compare what's in their hand to what's on the chart paper or the page.

3. As you play, arrange all of the blocks in alphabetical order, as in the beginning of the book.

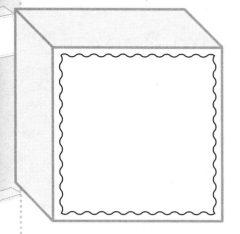

The letter _____ was found

_____

_____

_____.

By _____

# Chicka Chicka Boom Boom

### BY BILL MARTIN, JR. AND JOHN ARCHAMBAULT, ILLUSTRATED BY LOIS EHLERT

### (SIMON & SCHUSTER, 1989)

## Concepts and Themes

* Lowercase Letters
* Letter Names
* Rhyme & Rhythm

The lowercase letters are causing all kinds of trouble in the coconut tree! This rhythmic text, hot, tropical colors, and bold shapes combine into one perfect alphabet classic.

### Before Reading

Begin by sharing experiences of coconuts and climbing trees. Ask:

* Who here has climbed a tree?
* Can a person climb all the way to the very top of a tree? Why or why not?
* Have you ever seen a coconut tree? What did it look like?
* Have you ever eaten a coconut or tasted coconut milk? (You might bring in a coconut to examine, crack, and share with the group.)

Show children the cover of the book and read the title out loud. Ask them to repeat the title after you and practice chanting it.

### During Reading

* Read aloud with any rhythm that feels right to you. There is a CD with several chanted and musical versions available, but your own rendition of the text will work fine!
* Point to the colorful lowercase letters on each page as their names come up in the text.

### After Reading

* Read the book again, this time inviting children to chant "Chicka Chicka Boom Boom" whenever you give a signal (such as cupping your hand to your ear). Invite children to snap their fingers or tap their feet as you read.
* Act out the story and begin by having 26 letter blocks on the floor in front of you. Put the blocks up on a table or shelf to enact what is happening in the story, balancing them precariously, then knocking them down (or having a child do so) when they topple in the book. Have children yell "Boom! Boom!"

## Climb the Coconut Palm Tree

Invite children to act out the story with their very own palm tree!

1. Photocopy the tree pattern on page 43, enlarging it, if possible. Color as desired and then cut out the tree.

2. Tape the tree to a steel cookie sheet. Gather a set of uppercase and lowercase magnetic letters.

3. Read aloud *Chicka Chicka Boom Boom*. As you read the first part of the story, invite volunteers to place the magnetic letters on or around the tree as each letter's name is read.

4. Children then remove each letter in turn as you read the second part of the book.

5. To extend learning, record the story on an audiotape or CD and place in a listening center together with the cookie sheet and magnetic letters. Invite children to visit the center independently or in pairs to listen to the story and repeat the activity.

## Mamas and Papas, Uncles and Aunts

(Letter Formation, Letter Recognition, Reading Comprehension)

In this story, the lowercase letters are rescued by the uppercase letters—a great opportunity to discuss the differences between the two letter forms.

1. Together, examine the page that has the uppercase "mamas and papas and uncles and aunts" protectively gathering up the lowercase letters. Ask what is happening on the page (the uppercase letters *Z, R, J* and *N* are finding their lowercase versions and grabbing onto them or holding them).

2. Use the letter cards on pages 8–12 to play a "Mamas and Papas, Uncles and Aunts" game. For children's reference, display the beginning or ending spread of the book in which all letters are paired.

3. Distribute one card to each child (tackling half the alphabet at a time, such as *A–M*, then *N–Z* ) and tell the lowercase letters to lie down. The "uppercase letters" will "rescue" their matches, as in the book, and help the "lowercase letters" stand up. Children stay in pairs to show the rest of the group their matches. (Children show their cards and say, for instance, "I'm uppercase *A* and I rescued my baby, lowercase *a*," or "I'm lowercase *a*, and my aunt, uppercase *A*, helped me.")

Spotlight On . . .

*L M N O P*

The traditional alphabet song can make the letters *l, m, n, o,* and *p* sound like one letter ("elemenopee"), causing some children confusion. Take this opportunity to examine the five different letters that make up this "chunk" of the alphabet. Look at the page that reads "Chicka Chicka Boom Boom! Will there be enough room? Look who's coming! *L M N O P* !" Invite children to say the letter names as you point to each one. (Point to the letters in random order to check that children can recognize and name each letter.)

## Literature Links

**Barn Dance!**
by Bill Martin, Jr. and John Archambault, illustrated by Ted Rand
(Henry Holt and Co., 1988)

There's magic in the air when a quiet evening becomes a festival of foot-stompin', barn-dancin' fun. Another engaging blend of words and pictures from the *Chicka Chicka Boom Boom* creators.

**Boom Chicka Rock**
By John Archambault, illustrated by Suzanne Chitwood
(Philomel, 2004)

More chickas and more booms! The refrain "Boom Chicka Rock, Chicka Rock, Chicka Boom!" will have children moving to the rhythm of this story, in which mice party at midnight.

**Chicka Chicka 1, 2, 3**
by Bill Martin, Jr. and Michael Sampson, illustrated by Lois Ehlert
(Simon & Schuster, 2004)

*"1 told 2 and 2 told 3, 'I'll race you to the top of the apple tree.'"* The cut-paper art in this book is reminiscent of *Chicka Chicka Boom Boom*, down to the vibrant splashes of color. Numbers ascend by ones up to 20, then switch to intervals of tens (30, 40, 50) up to 100. This book is a great choice for 100th Day of School activities.

# Look Who's Coming!

(Letter Formation, Letter Recognition, Letter Names, Social Studies)

Focusing on the letters in children's names is a great way to develop letter recognition and build classroom community at the same time.

1. Photocopy page 43 for each child. Tell children that they *all* belong in the coconut tree—all of the letters in their names, that is! Explain that they are going to create their own class book.

2. Demonstrate how to complete the page. Children use crayons and markers. If children can't yet write their first names, they can copy from a model.

3. Gather all of the pages together and bind into a class book. Create a cover with a title, such as "Chicka Chicka Kindergarten." Read it together, asking children to identify the letters on each page. (The child who created each page might read his or her own page to the group.)

4. For added fun, draw a coconut tree shape on chart paper and write all of the letters that appear in children's names at the top of the tree, using the same bright colors as in the book.

# Chicka Chicka Yum, Yum

Invite children to make their own palm tree snacks—and celebrate letters!

**Ingredients** (for each child)

- celery stalk
- lettuce leaf
- cream cheese (tinted with green food coloring)
- alphabet-shaped cereal

1. Give each child a paper plate. Have children assemble a "palm tree" using a celery stalk "trunk" and pieces of lettuce torn into leaf shapes.

2. Let children use plastic knives to spread cream cheese on the trunk and dab some on the leaves.

3. Spread out several handfuls of alphabet-shaped cereal on paper towels. Let children take turns examining and identifying the letters. Then let each child choose some of the letters to press onto their trees. (Children might choose their initials or letters to spell simple words.)

# Look who's coming!

The letters _____.

_____'s on the way up the coconut tree.

# The Butterfly Alphabet

### BY KJELL B. SANDVED

### (SCHOLASTIC, 1996)

*"To find beauty in the world, you have to look closely."*
—Kjell B. Sandved

## Concepts and Themes

* Letter Shapes
* Looking Closely
* Science & Nature
* Colors, Shapes & Patterns

Many years ago, nature photographer Kjell B. Sandved was looking at a tropical moth through a microscope. To his surprise, he saw a tiny, perfect letter *F* on its wing. He spent the next 25 years traveling the world, finding and photographing the entire alphabet spelled out on the wings of butterflies and moths. His luminous book celebrates the intricate and amazing patterns and shapes on these delicate creatures, which display nature's very own alphabet. Letters really are everywhere!

### Before Reading

Begin by finding out what children already know about butterflies, building their interest and sharing fun facts. Ask:

* Where have you seen a butterfly? What do you think is special about butterflies?

* How do butterflies begin life? (*egg, caterpillar, chrysalis*)

* What is the difference between a butterfly and a moth? (*Moths are nocturnal, butterflies are not; butterflies' bodies are thin, moths' are thick.*)

* Why do you think butterflies are brightly colored? (*They use their colors to recognize each other and to camouflage—hide themselves—to keep safe from enemies, such as birds.*)

* How big do you think the biggest butterfly is? (*one foot wide*) The smallest? (*less than one half inch*)

* What do you think butterfly and moth wings are made from? (*thousands of tiny overlapping scales, like sequins or shingles on a roof*)

Introduce the concept of finding familiar shapes in surprising places by holding up your right hand in an *L* shape so the group can see. Ask, "What letter do you see in my hand?" Explain that the book you will share has letters in unexpected places, too. Show children the cover of the book and ask what they think they might see inside.

## During Reading

❋ Read the rhyme on each page aloud, emphasizing the word printed in a different color. Emphasize the beginning sound that corresponds to the letter on the butterfly.

❋ Invite children to name the letter they see on the right-hand page, and to examine the smaller picture of the butterfly on the left side to find the letter.

❋ Try having children air-trace each letter as you look at that page.

## After Reading

Page through the book again, pointing out the names of different butterflies. You might choose a few to focus on each time you reread.

❋ Invite children to come up and use their fingers to trace the letter shape right on the page. (You might choose children whose first or last names begin with that letter.)

❋ Ask children whether the letter is uppercase or lowercase. Write each letter on chart paper and include the one that is not pictured on the page. For instance, on the first page, uppercase *A* is shown, but not lowercase *a*. Write uppercase *A* on the chart paper, then write lowercase *a* next to it.

❋ Discuss unfamiliar words children encounter in the text, such as *radiant*, *nectar*, and *ease*.

## Extending Learning

## Butterfly Symmetry (Letter Formation, Letter Recognition, Math, Art)

Children can make their very own fluttering butterflies—using letters.

1. Copy page 11 of *The Butterfly Alphabet* and page 48 of this book for each child.

2. Explain that some letters (*A, I, i, l, M, O, o, T, t, U, V, v, W, w, X, x, Y*) are symmetrical: you can draw a line dividing them into two matching halves. Butterflies are symmetrical, too!

3. Invite each child to choose a letter (or several letters) from the list above to paint on *one* wing of a butterfly with tempera paint (use several colors), using a cotton swab as a paintbrush.

4. Have children fold their butterflies in half along the center dashed line, press firmly, then unfold. When children open their butterflies, they will see that the wings match on both sides— they are symmetrical.

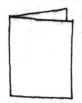

The letter won't always be easily visible, but children might take turns later with a plastic magnifying glass in the science center.

Spotlight On...

Letter Oo

Some butterfly or moth wings have eyespots: bright, round dots or circles. They are meant to scare away other animals that may eat them (such as bats, birds, frogs, or monkeys). Point out that the letter *Oo* is round, too. Look at the *O* page. How many circles do children see?

## Looking for Letters

(Letter Recognition, Letter Formation, Letter Names)

Letters are everywhere! Challenge children to go on a "letter hunt."

1. Have each child use his pencil and writing journal (or clipboard and paper).

2. Tell children to spend a few minutes working in pairs, walking around to find and record "hidden letters" around the room. For instance, they might see an uppercase *H* in the pane of a window, or an uppercase *N* in three books leaning on a bookshelf.

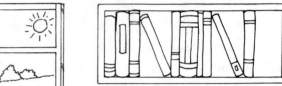

3. Invite children to share their findings with the group.

## Butterfly Ballet

(Movement, Dramatic Play, Reading Comprehension)

When children need a break or an energy release, invite them to flit and flutter like butterflies!

1. Have children stand up. Explain that you are going to read the rhymes on each page and they are going to act them out. You might put on classical music to complete the scenario.

2. Read each rhyme slowly and rhythmically as children "become" butterflies. You will be the narrator of their story.

3. Encourage children to act out as much "butterfly ballet" as they can: "sipping nectar," "soaring," "quickly flitting," and so on. (Not every rhyme corresponds to an exact movement that children can do, but the overall poetry and sing-song quality of the text will enchant nonetheless.)

## Color & Glimmer Letter Pages

(Art, Letter Recognition, Letter Formation)

Children can add their own color and sparkle to butterfly wings.

1. Use a black and white copier to copy some of the butterfly wings in the book (the right-hand pages only). You may need to experiment with different amounts of darkness. The result should be a black and white page in which the letter shape is clear enough for children to interact with.

2. Set the pages out in the art center (and/or the writing center) for children to color in themselves using crayons. They should first trace the letter, then color in or decorate the rest of the wing.

3. Help children use a cotton swab to trace over the letter in glue, then sprinkle glitter onto the letter. Shake off excess glitter and let dry for a shimmering "letter wing"!

## Butterflies and Moths (Math, Science, Vocabulary, Letter Recognition)

Explore the similarities and differences between butterflies and moths.

1. Look in the back of the book for information about the differences between butterflies and moths. Read it aloud to the group.

2. Compare the *J* page (Blume's Swallowtail Butterfly) with the *W* page (Geometrid Moth). Point out the differences between the two (*butterfly has a thin body, moth has a thick body, butterfly has bright colors, moth has dull colors*).

3. Use two hula hoops to create a giant Venn diagram. (You can also use yarn or string to create two large overlapping circles.) On 17 index cards, write the following words and phrases, then place the index cards reading "Butterflies" and "Moths" above or below each circle and "Both" above or below the intersection of the circles.

4. Read each index card aloud to the group and ask, "Does this describe butterflies, moths, or both?" Discuss where in the Venn diagram it belongs. Invite a volunteer to lay the index card in the appropriate section.

### Butterflies
- Begins with *B*
- Have thin bodies
- Busy during day
- Use eyes
- Bright colors

### Moths
- Begins with *M*
- Have thick bodies
- Busy at nighttime
- Use nose
- Dull colors

### Both
- Have wings
- Have tiny scales on wings
- Insects
- Begin life as eggs, then caterpillar, then chrysalis

## Literature Links

***The Beetle Alphabet Book***
by Jerry Pallotta, illustrated by David Biedrzycki (Charlesbridge, 2004)

Bugs appear alphabetically in huge computer-generated illustrations that zoom in on every pincer and shell spot.

***Peterson First Guide to Butterflies and Moths***
by Paul A. Opler, illustrated by Amy Bartlett Wright (Houghton Mifflin Harcourt, 1998)

A great first field guide to include in your science center.

***Where Butterflies Grow***
by Joanne Ryder, illustrated by Lynne Cherry (Puffin, 1996)

Follow the amazing odyssey from egg to caterpillar to chrysalis to butterfly. Children can also sharpen their powers of observation by finding the tiny creatures hiding on each page.

## Teaching Tip

See page 34 for another Venn diagram activity.

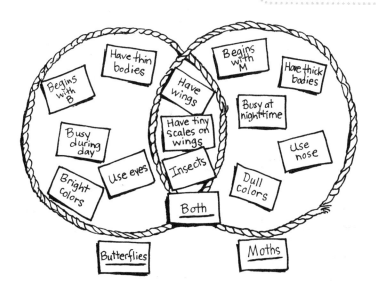

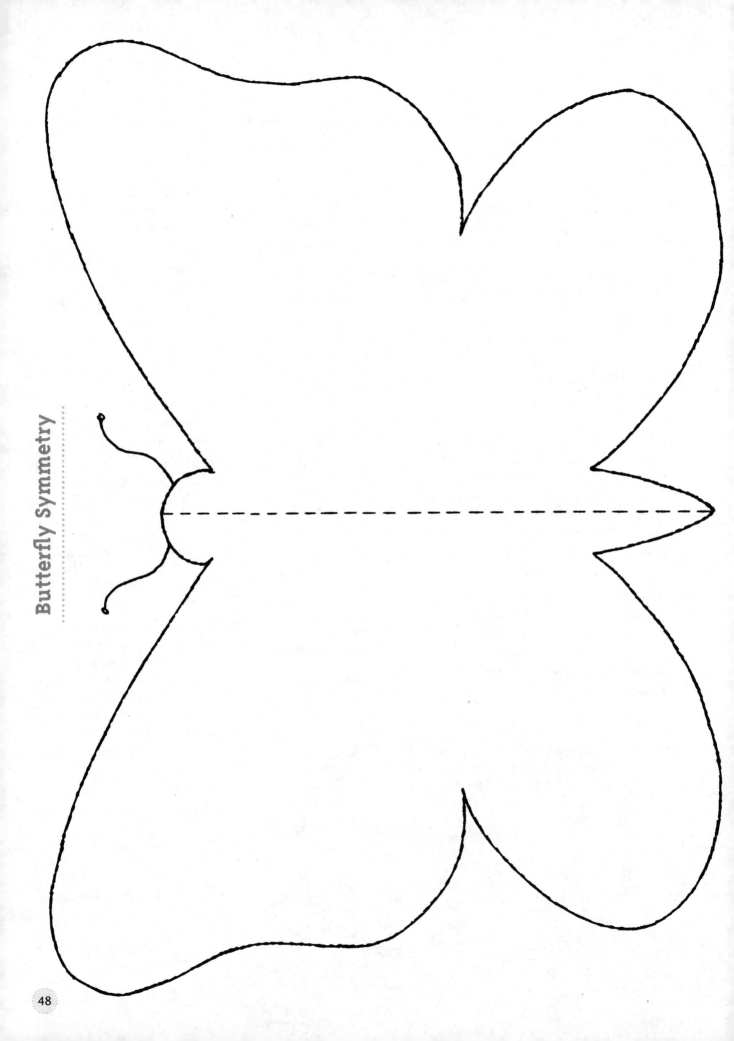

Butterfly Symmetry

# Eating the Alphabet:
## Fruits and Vegetables From A to Z

### By Lois Ehlert

### (Harcourt, 1989)

Lois Ehlert's signature cut-paper collage style has become a classroom favorite. This book celebrates vibrant vegetables, succulent fruits, and nature's bounty in general—all in alphabetical order.

## Concepts and Themes

- ❋ Healthy Eating
- ❋ Uppercase and Lowercase Letters
- ❋ Colors

## Before Reading

Begin by building children's interest in fruits and vegetables and sharing experiences. Ask:

- ❋ What is your favorite fruit? What are some fruits that are red? How about yellow? (Continue with different colors.)

- ❋ What is your favorite vegetable? What are some vegetables that are green? How about orange? (Continue with different colors.)

- ❋ Who has visited a farmer's market? What did you see there?

- ❋ Has anyone ever picked fruits or vegetables themselves? How was it growing—on a vine, on a tree, or in the ground?

- ❋ What is the difference between fruits and vegetables? (The fruit of a plant contains its seeds: apples, pears, peaches, oranges, bananas, mangoes, kiwis, and even cucumbers and tomatoes are all fruits. Vegetables include everything else: the leaves, stalks, stems [including tubers], and roots.)

## During Reading

- ❋ Point to each picture as you say its name, emphasizing the beginning sound of the target word.

- ❋ Say, for instance, "*A* is for . . ." and point to the artichoke. Children complete your sentence by saying *artichoke*. Then point to the avocado and say "*A* is for . . ." Children complete the sentence: *avocado*.

- ❋ Point out that each word is shown twice, once in all lowercase and once in all uppercase.

## Letter Pp

Look at how many fruits and vegetables begin with *Pp*! Examine the *Pp* pages closely: there's *papaya, parsnip, pea, peach, pear, pepper, persimmon, pineapple, plum, pomegranate, potato,* and *pumpkin.* Share *Each Peach Pear Plum* by Janet and Allen Ahlberg (Viking, 1979) for more fruity fun with the letter *Pp.* Challenge children to find all the peaches, pears, and plums on the cover.

## After Reading

❉ Do children show particular interest in a specific fruit or vegetable? Which are new to them? Check out the endnotes to learn more about each fruit and vegetable pictured in the book.

❉ Hide different fruits and vegetables in paper bags or boxes. (Show them the fruits or vegetables that you are putting into the bags or boxes first, so they have some sense of what might be inside.) Let children reach into the bag and describe what they feel. Help them use descriptive words such as *long, short, soft, hard, smooth, round, thin, thick,* and so on. Can they identify what they are touching?

## Extending Learning

### Taste Test (Vocabulary, Math, Letter Recognition)

Introduce new healthy foods and create a simple graph.

1. Choose several fruits or vegetables that not all children have tasted (or seen in their original form) before. Let them watch you cut each open and into small pieces.

2. Set them out on separate plates so each child can taste one (check for food allergies first). Taste one at a time and discuss its qualities: chewy, crispy, sweet, sour, bitter, and so on.

3. Have children vote for their favorite and record their responses on a bar graph.

4. Examine the graph together. What was their favorite?

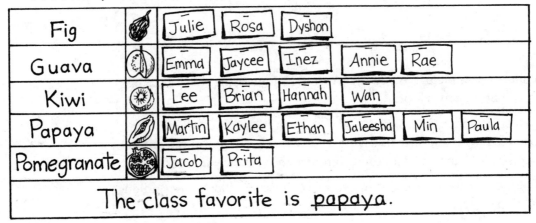

## What Fruit Does Our Class Like Best?

| Fig | | Julie | Rosa | Dyshon | | |
|---|---|---|---|---|---|---|
| Guava | | Emma | Jaycee | Inez | Annie | Rae |
| Kiwi | | Lee | Brian | Hannah | Wan | |
| Papaya | | Martin | Kaylee | Ethan | Jaleesha | Min | Paula |
| Pomegranate | | Jacob | Prita | | | |

The class favorite is papaya.

# Eating the Rainbow (Art, Vocabulary)

*Eating the Alphabet* is full of crisp, vibrant colors. Children can create their own watercolor cut-paper fruits and vegetables while practicing fine motor skills.

1. Divide the class into groups at four different tables with a large sheet of white butcher paper in the middle of each table. Each group will be responsible for covering their butcher paper in a different color of watercolor paint: one for the colors orange and yellow, one for green, one for blue and purple, and one for red. Provide several different shades of each color and encourage children to cover their paper with paint, experimenting with using more and less water.

2. Let the large sheets dry and cut them into smaller squares that children can easily cut with their own scissors.

3. Let children create their own fruits and vegetables. Demonstrate by cutting out a simple shape, such as a carrot. Children can also look at the pages of the book for inspiration. Then have them use glue sticks to adhere their colorful fruit and vegetables to sheets of white paper. Help children label their creations, then make an "Eating the Alphabet" display for all to enjoy.

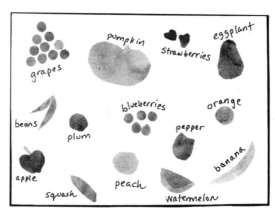

# Friendship Fruit Salad

(Letter Recognition, Phonemic Awareness, Cooking, Social Studies)

Children can make their own sweet snack with fruits from A to Z.

1. Invite each child to bring in one piece of any kind of fruit. Have them show their fruit to the group. Write its name on chart paper. Ask, "What letter (or sound) does it start with? Does this fruit appear in the book?"

2. Children can watch as you chop each fruit and place in a large bowl. Let children take turns gently stirring the fruit together.

3. Enjoy the snack together. (You might serve with yogurt.) Discuss how we all have our own favorite tastes, but we can enjoy them together. We can all be very different, but we make up one big group.

## Literature Links

Lois Ehlert is a great subject for an author study. Check out *Teaching With Favorite Lois Ehlert Books* by Pamela Chanko (Scholastic, 2005).

### Growing Vegetable Soup
By Lois Ehlert
(Harcourt, 1987)

Using her characteristically vibrant palette, Ehlert details the raising of a vegetable garden to make "the best soup ever." She even includes a recipe for vegetable soup!

### Planting a Rainbow
By Lois Ehlert
(Voyager, 1992)

A dazzling celebration of the colors in a flower garden.

### Red Leaf, Yellow Leaf
By Lois Ehlert
(Harcourt, 1991)

Witness the beginning of a sugar maple's life from the point of view of a young child. Besides the tree itself, Ehlert includes several varieties of birds and gardening tools.

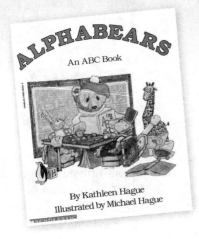

# Alphabears: An ABC Book

## BY KATHLEEN HAGUE, ILLUSTRATED BY MICHAEL HAGUE

### (HENRY HOLT, 1984)

## Concepts and Themes

❋ Teddy Bears

❋ First Names

❋ Personalities & Traits

Letter learning doesn't get much cuter or cuddlier than *Alphabears*. Introduce children to a menagerie of adorable teddy bears with names ranging from Amanda to Zak, each with its own personality and alliterative tendencies (for instance, "G is for Gilbert, a gruff grizzly bear/Whenever he growls you'd better beware").

### Before Reading

Begin by building children's interest in teddy bears. Ask:

❋ Who here has a teddy bear? What is his or her name?

❋ Whose first name begins with *B*? (Repeat with last names.) How about *T*?

❋ Has anyone read a book about *Winnie the Pooh*? How about other bear stories, such as *Goldilocks and The Three Bears, Corduroy*, or *The Berenstain Bears*? (Other fictional bears that some children may have heard of include Paddington Bear, The Carebears, Smokey the Bear, Yogi the Bear, and Fozzie Bear.)

❋ What do you think this book will be about? (Show children the cover of the book. Explain that they will be meeting an entire alphabet of teddy bears.)

### During Reading

❋ Read the couplet on each page aloud, emphasizing the letter that appears on the page and the name of that teddy bear (for instance, *N is for Nikki*).

❋ Often, children will be able to complete the rhyme. (For instance, when you read "P is for Pam, who loves a parade/She also likes popcorn and pink lemon...," children finish the rhyme with "-ade!")

### After Reading

❋ Who were children's favorite bears in the story?

❋ Discuss unfamiliar words children encounter in the text, such as *gruff, soars,* and *ease.*

## Teddy Bear Picnic

(Letter Formation, Letter Recognition, Letter Names, Phonemic Awareness)

Children form letter shapes out of teddy bear graham crackers at snack time.

1. Using a marker, write letters you wish to target on paper plates (one or two large letters per plate). You can include uppercase, lowercase, or both. The number of plates will depend on your class size.

2. At snack time, set out the plates and a bowl of teddy-bear shaped graham crackers. Children place the crackers on the marker lines to form letters.

3. Have children examine and discuss the names and sounds of each other's letters. Then have a teddy bear picnic!

## Alphabears Quilt

(Letter Formation, Reading Comprehension, Math)

Invite children to create their "beary" own quilt.

1. Photocopy page 55 for each child and help children complete it.

2. Arrange the pages together on a bulletin board with the title "Snuggle Up With Our ABC's." Discuss how to arrange the pages into one large square. How many rows of how many pages will make up a square (or rectangle)? For instance, if you have 25 students, you can make a five-by-five grid.

## Bear Names (Letter Recognition, Phonemic Awareness, Letter Names)

Children's names are a great opportunity for letter learning.

1. Write the alphabet down one side of a sheet of chart paper. Read the book again. As you read each page, stop and complete each bear's name on the chart paper. (Use a different color than you used for the initial letter.)

2. As you write each name, say aloud the names of the letters in it. Then stretch out the sounds so children can hear how the names are made up of different sounds.

3. Compare the bears' names to the names in your group. Does anyone have the same name as one of the bears?

4. Write children's names in a different color next to their corresponding letters.

Spotlight On . . .

Letter Qq

*Q* is for *quilt*! Together, examine the *Q* page: "Q is for Quimbly, a soft quilted bear/Who was sewn by hand with much love and care." Discuss quilts. Make a list of other words that start with Q. Explain that *Q* is usually followed by a *u: quiet, queen, quarter, quack, quail.*

# Teddy Bear, Teddy Bear, Turn Around

(Letter Recognition, Letter Formation, Following Directions, Movement)

Certain letters are easy for individual children to form with their bodies. Combine this simple activity with a favorite rhyme.

1. Have children stand up and follow your chanted directions:

   Teddy bear, teddy bear, turn around.
   Teddy bear, teddy bear, touch the ground.
   Teddy bear, teddy bear, make a/an _____*!

   * These letters are the simplest for individual children to make with their bodies: C, F, L (children should sit down on the floor to form L), I, P, T, and Y. Write the target letter on chart paper for children to use as a model.

2. Children stand in place, turn around, and touch the ground according to the rhyme, then become the letter you name.

# B Is for Bear Biscuits (Cooking, Phonemic Awareness)

This snack will satisfy even a bear's appetite!

1. Give each child two uncooked round refrigerator biscuits (available in tubes) and a square of foil. Have them place one whole biscuit on the foil to represent a bear's head.

2. Have children tear the second biscuit in half. One half they should roll into a ball and place in the center of the bear's head to create a snout. The other half they should divide into two pieces, and press on top of the bear's head to form ears.

3. Give each child three raisins and invite them to press them into the dough to make two eyes and the tip of the bear's nose. They can then sprinkle their biscuits with cinnamon sugar. Use a permanent marker to write children's initials on their foil squares.

4. Place the biscuits (on the foil squares) on a cookie sheet and bake according to the package directions. When cool, give the bears back to the children who made them.

5. Invite each child to give his or her bear a name and tell the group what it is. Repeat the name, emphasizing the first letter and its sound ("Your bear's name is Roy? What letter does Roy start with? What sound does *R* make?")

Name _____ Date _____

Make your own bear. What is its name? What does he or she like to do?

_____ is for _____ ,

who _____

_____ .

# Into the A, B, Sea

### By Deborah Lee Rose, illustrated by Steve Jenkins

### (Scholastic, 2000)

**S**plash! It's an exhilarating dive into an ocean of letters and rhyming text. On each page of this gorgeous book, sea creatures of every shape, size, and color exemplify every letter of the alphabet.

## Concepts and Themes

* Underwater Habitats
* Sea Creatures
* Action Words

### Before Reading

Begin by building children's interest in underwater life. Ask:

* What does it feel like to be under water?
* How can you see when you are under water?
* What happens if you open your eyes under water? If you are wearing goggles, what might you see?
* What lives under water?
* Would you like to live under water?

### During Reading

* Read the phrase on each page aloud, emphasizing the beginning sound of the target words.
* Let children examine the illustrations on each page.

### After Reading

* How many creatures can children recall? Make a list on chart paper of what they remember. Can they remember what the creatures were doing in the book?
* Are there any creatures in the book children are particularly curious about? Refer to the last page of the book for more information about each sea creature.
* Page through the book again, discussing unfamiliar words children encounter in the text, such as *cling, prance,* and *slumber.* Invite them to act those words out.

## Sea Creature Match Up (Letter Recognition, Vocabulary, Movement)

Children enact their own underwater movement festival based on the words they recognize and read.

1. Read through the book again, and as you encounter these animals and verbs, write them on index cards (one word per card): *anemones/sting, barnacles/cling, crabs/crawl, flying fish/soar, humpbacks/leap, insects/prance, jellies/dance, kelp forests/sway, octopuses/hide, penguins/glide.*

2. Distribute one card to each child. When you say "go," challenge children to find their match and sit side by side in a circle. Children can refer to the book to check their matches.

3. Each pair shows and acts out their word cards to the group. (For instance, the pair with *anemones sting* says, "We are anemones. We sting," and pantomimes stinging.)

**Spotlight On... Letter Ss**

*S* is for *sand* and *sea!* Pass around a piece of sandpaper. What is it used for? (to *smooth out wood*) Using a permanent marker, trace a large *S* onto a piece of sandpaper and invite children to trace it with their fingers to enhance tactile learning. You might also fill one third of a reasealable plastic bag with sand, then close tightly. Or use blue finger paint to make a blue sea in a bag. (Use duct tape to ensure a tight seal.) Tape a sheet of white paper to one side of the bag. Then let children use their fingers to practice writing the letter *s* in the sand or paint. (The white paper helps the letter show up better.)

## Underwater Alphabet Bulletin Board (Art, Letter Recognition)

Bring the wonder above ground and right into your classroom.

1. Look through the pages of the book again. Assign each child a different animal to illustrate, using crayons, markers, or colored pencils.

2. When they have finished drawing, children cut out their creatures. Staple them all onto a bulletin board with a blue background.

3. Help children create labels for their creatures, using markers and index cards or slips of paper. Use a different color to emphasize the beginning letters. Display the labels next to the creatures.

4. Title the bulletin board "Into the A, B, Sea" and display the book nearby.

## Bodies of Water (Letter Formation, Letter Recognition, Movement)

Children can work together to form letters with their bodies. This is great for kinesthetic learners!

1. Have children stand in a circle. Together, spread a green or blue blanket or sheet in the center of the circle to indicate "ocean."

2. Then call out any letter (upper- or lowercase or both, depending on your group's level) and challenge three (or more, if you are doing both upper- and lowercase) children at a time to work together to lie down and form that letter on the sheet. (For children's reference, write the letter on the board, on a sheet of chart paper, or refer to an alphabet frieze in the room).

## Go Fish for Letters

(Letter Recognition, Letter Formation, Phonemic Awareness, Vocabulary)

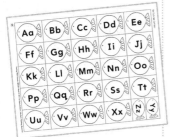

Build letter-recognition skills and fine motor-skills at the same time.

1. In advance, make a "fishing rod" by tying string to a dowel. Then tie a magnet to the end of the string. (Depending on the magnet's size and shape, you may need to glue the string to the magnet or use masking tape.)

2. Enlarge and photocopy page 60 and cut apart the fish patterns. Attach a paper clip to each fish.

3. Gather children in a circle and show them the fish. Place the fish facedown in the center of the circle. (For added fun, place the fish in a wading pool or large tub.)

4. Let children take turns "fishing" for letters. When they catch one, they show it to the group and say its letter name. Turn back to the corresponding page in the book to look at the animal it represents.

5. Emphasize the letter's sound and, on chart paper, make a list together of words and names beginning with that sound. Demonstrate how the letter is formed, then invite children to trace the letter shape in the air or on the floor with their fingers.

## Underwater Charades (Movement, Dramatic Play, Letter Recognition)

Create an underwater drama filled with action words!

1. To reinforce letter sounds, page through the book again and stop where you see two letters on facing pages. (For example, the *I* and *J* spread shows *Insects prance* and *Jellies dance*).

2. Divide the group in half and assign one letter to each group. Write the two letters on chart paper so you can point to them easily.

3. Point to either of the letters, and that group acts out their animal's action (the *I*'s prance like insects, the *J*'s dance and wiggle like jellies). Switch back and forth quickly!

## P Is for Paper

(Letter Recognition, Letter Names, Art, Vocabulary, Science)

The art in *Into the A, B, Sea* is made from a variety of beautifully cut paper. Explore ways paper is used, then make paper collages and help build fine-motor skills.

1. Examine the pages of the book closely. Let children get up close to each page to see the art. Each picture is made from cut paper in different colors, thicknesses, and textures.

2. Write the word *Paper* on chart paper. Ask, "How many *p*'s are in the word? (*one uppercase, one lowercase*) What is paper used for?" (*books, notebooks, magazines, blank sheets to write and draw on, packaging*).

3. Gather paper in a wide variety of colors and textures and pass it around for children to examine and discuss. (You can ask a local stationery or paper store for scraps or irregular pieces, or ask families to bring in different types of paper.) Use words to describe it, such as *soft, smooth, rough, velvety, glossy, silky, shiny, dull, thick, thin*.

4. Cut all the paper into smaller pieces (about 3-inch squares). Then set out all the squares at the art table.

5. Have children use scissors to cut the paper into any shapes they wish and glue it onto one sheet of paper to create a paper collage. Help them label their collages "P Is for Paper."

### Literature Links

**One Nighttime Sea**
By Deborah Lee Rose, illustrated by Steve Jenkins (Scholastic, 2003)

More vivid cut-paper collages from the creators of *Into the A, B, Sea!*, this time focusing on numbers. Lyrical text lets children count sea creatures going about their evening activities.

**O Is for Oystercatcher: A Book of Seaside ABCs**
by Barbara Patrizzi (Down the Shore Publishers, 2003)

This book of beautiful, wood-block prints portrays a variety of seashore birds and wildlife, with fascinating tidbits of information accompanying the pictures. (Did you know seahorses do not have stomachs, but consume up to 250 shrimp per hour?)

**The Underwater Alphabet Book**
by Jerry Pallotta, illustrated by Edgar Stewart Charlesbridge Publishing (May 1991)

Jerry Pallotta's fact-filled alphabet books cover myriad themes; this one focuses on the coral reef ecosystem. From *Angelfish* to *Zebra Pipefish*, meet an alphabet of amazing tropical creatures.

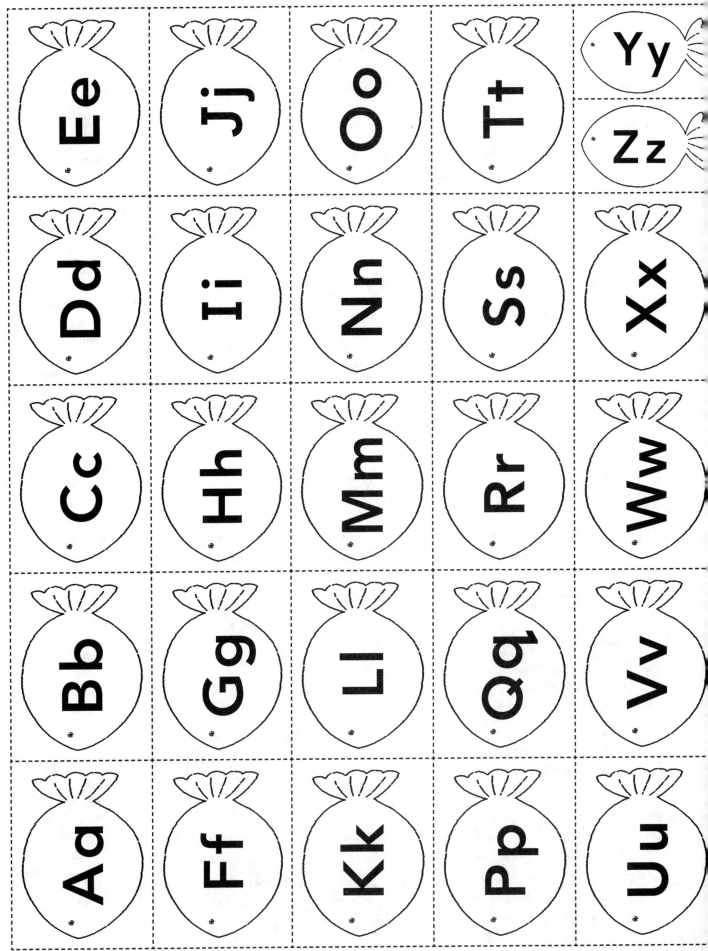

# Alphabet Adventure

## BY AUDREY WOOD AND BRUCE WOOD

## (SCHOLASTIC, 2001)

This book veers away from the typical alphabet book format of one letter per page. Instead, it's an ingenious tale of the entire alphabet working as a team. When little *i* loses his dot, it's up to all the other letters to help find it so that they can all go to school to help a child learn his *ABC's*. And that dot is hiding on each page, waiting for readers to find it!

### Before Reading

Show children the cover of the book and read the title aloud. Ask:

❋ What do you see on the cover of this book?

❋ What do you think will happen in this book?

❋ What kind of adventure might the alphabet go on?

❋ Have you ever gone on an adventure? What was it?

❋ Would you like to be on this boat with all of these letters?

### During Reading

❋ Read the book aloud, pointing out certain letters in the illustration as necessary or inviting children to find the letters themselves.

❋ Let children examine each page closely. Challenge them to find the dot hiding on each page. The dot is even hiding on the very last page of the book! What other details do they notice?

### After Reading

❋ Ask, "Why is the teacher named Capital T?" (*Teacher begins with* T.)

❋ Ask, "What other letter uses a dot like *i*?" (*j*) "Why are the dots important?" (*They're part of the letters.*)

❋ Discuss unfamiliar words children encounter in the text, such as *canal, crumple,* and *proper.*

## Concepts and Themes

❋ Lowercase and Uppercase Letters

❋ Teamwork

❋ Letter Sequence

❋ Noticing Detail

*T* is for *teacher* and *teamwork*! In this story, Capital T teaches the entire lowercase alphabet to work as a team and get in the right order. Have children find the capital *T* on each page. (It appears on most pages but not all.) Demonstrate how to form uppercase *T* on chart paper or the board. (You can present lowercase *t* as well.) Make a list of other words that begin with *T* (*two, turtle, tea, ten, towel, toe, tent, turkey, time*, etc.).

> ### Extending Learning

## Flying Yellow Pencil (Letter Sequence, Letter Names)

Build children's understanding of letter sequence right into transition times.

**1.** Together, read and examine the spread in which the letters climb aboard the yellow pencil and take off!

**2.** What do children notice about the flying pencil? (*The letters are all in a row in order, with the capital* T *teacher at the head of the line at the eraser end, and the point of the pencil at the front, as if ready to write!*) What else do they notice? (*There are other pencils flying and landing, each with an alphabet and a capital* Teacher.)

**3.** When it's time to line up to leave your classroom, call out one child at a time to get into line. The first child you call says "a" as he or she walks to begin the line. The second child you call says "b," joins hands with, and stands behind "a," and so on, until all children are lined up.

## Dot, Dot, Dot (Phonemic Awareness, Letter Recognition)

Here's a great opportunity to focus on beginning sounds.

**1.** Capital *I* had a plan for all the letters to choose an object that could substitute for *I*'s dot. Turn to the spread in which each letter picks an object that corresponds to its sound.

**2.** Point to each letter and have children call out the name of its object. (For instance, point to *b* and say, "The *b* chose a . . .," and children call out "bug!")

**3.** Look at the next spread, on which *s* offers a star, *h* offers a heart, *b* offers a bug, and *c* offers a cherry. Turn back a page and ask children what other letters brought objects that might have made good dots for *i* (*e* brought an egg, *l* brought a light bulb, *o* brought an orange).

## Alphabet Island (Movement, Letter Recognition, Phonemic Awareness)

Children create their very own alphabet island—and catch a boat to get off!

1. Assign one child to be the "boat." Give all children except the boat one letter card. Have them stand together on an "island" (a rug or another clearly delineated area). The boat stands apart.

2. Tell children they are all letters and they are going to travel to a place they are really needed—in books. The object of the game is to get all letters to the library corner or reading area.

3. One by one, call out letter names and sounds. Depending on children's level, give other clues such as "This letter is the first letter in the word ___," or "This letter begins _____'s name." The child holding that letter holds it up, and the "boat" escorts the child to the library corner or reading area.

4. Once everyone has reached the library corner or reading area, gather the cards and read a book!

## Straighten Up!

(Letter Formation, Letter Recognition, Letter Names, Letter Sequence)

Help children reinforce their understanding of letter orientation.

1. Turn to the spread in which the entire alphabet is all out of order, standing every which way. (*The little letters were so excited that many forgot their correct places. Some didn't face front or stand straight, and others turned upside down.*)

2. Read the text aloud again and tell children they are going to act like Capital T and help the letters get themselves straight.

3. Write a letter on chart paper in a way that needs correcting. You might write it upside down or sideways, with wiggly or crooked lines, or missing a part (such as the dot on the *j*).

4. Children take the role of the Capital T and help the letters get themselves into the right position. Invite a volunteer to write the letter correctly next to its incorrect version.

5. You can also use letter cards to play this game. Have children sit in a circle and scatter the letter cards face up in all different directions. Children's task is to straighten them out and put them in alphabetical order.

### Literature Links

***Alphabet Mystery***
By Audrey Wood and
Bruce Wood
(Scholastic, 2003)

More clever letter fun from the creators of *Alphabet Adventure*. When Little x disappears from Charley's Alphabet, the rest of the letters search for him. But he doesn't want to be rescued—because he feels bad that Charley seldom uses him! How can little *x* find his place in the alphabet?

***Silly Sally***
By Audrey Wood
(Red Wagon Books, 2007)

The characters in Wood's zesty, sunny tale fairly jump off the page in this cumulative rhyme. Children will long to join Silly Sally and her outrageous friends as they parade into town!

***Word Builder***
By Ann Whitford Paul,
illustrated by Kurt Cyrus
(Simon & Schuster, 2009)

Letters make words, words make sentences, sentences make paragraphs, paragraphs make chapters, and chapters make books. This construction-themed book is a great introduction to concepts of print, and why and how people write.

Once your class has explored all of the alphabet books featured in this book (or however many you choose to share with them), you can celebrate children's letter learning with these culminating activities:

## ABC Bulletin Board

Create a bulletin board displaying every letter of the alphabet. (All three of the following ideas can be done with 26 small white paper plates.)

- **Superstar Letter Learners!:** Cover a bulletin board with black paper. Children can use watercolors to paint their plates to look like planets. Once dry, children write one letter on each plate. Attach the plates in ABC order to the bulletin board and add some paper stars for a sky full of letters.

- **Come to Our Alphabet Picnic:** Cover a bulletin board in red and white checkerboard paper or anything that might resemble a picnic blanket. Children write letters on the plates and attach them to the "blanket." Hot glue some plastic utensils and napkins to the board and you're ready for a picnic!

- **Letterpillar!:** Children can create and display all 26 paper plates with letters in an alphabetical row to form a caterpillar. (Use a separate one for the head.) Draw legs under each plate, and you've got a creepy crawly alphabet.

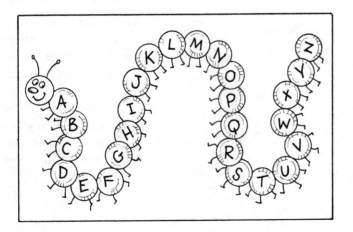

## Alphabet Frieze

Make an alphabet frieze to display. Assign each child a letter (depending on class size, some children may need to make more than one, or two children will need to work together on one). Have them write that letter (upper- and lowercase forms) on a sheet of paper and draw something beginning with that letter. As a group, put the letter pages in a row in alphabetical order, then attach to the wall at children's eye level.

## Dear Author

Do children have favorites among all the books you enjoyed? They can write letters to the authors and enjoy their websites. Here are six authors who are easy to contact:

✳ *Alphabet Adventure* by Audrey Wood

You'll find contact information and lots of kid-friendly activities at audreywood.com/mac_site/clubhouse/clubhouse_page/clubhouse.htm

✳ *The Butterfly Alphabet* by Kjell Sandved

On www.butterflyalphabet.com, children can browse through more beautiful images.

✳ *Chicka Chicka Boom Boom* by Bill Martin, Jr. and J. Archambault

Contact Bill Martin, Jr. on his website: billmartinjr.com

✳ *Into the A, B, Sea!* by Deborah Lee Rose

On the author's website, deborahleerose.com, children can write e-mails and look at her other books.

✳ *I Spy Letters* by Jean Marzollo and Walter Wick

Contact Jean Marzollo and Walter Wick on their websites: jeanmarzollo.com and walterwick.com

✳ *The Letters Are Lost* by Lisa Campbell Ernst

Post a message on the author's message board at authors.simonandschuster.com/Lisa-Campbell-Ernst/706370